Flying Saucers

'convincing and impressive.'

New Statesman

Plate 1 A UFO Vision (*frontispiece*)

Carl Gustav
Jung

Flying Saucers

A modern myth of things seen in the sky

 London and New York

*Ein moderner Mythus. Von dingen, die am Himmel
gesehen werden* first published 1958
by Rascher, Zurich

English edition first published 1959
by Routledge & Kegan Paul

First published in Routledge Classics 2002
by Routledge
2 Park Square, Milton Park, Abingdon, Oxon, OX14 4RN

*Routledge is an imprint of the Taylor & Francis Group,
An informa business*

Typeset in Joanna by RefineCatch Limited, Bungay, Suffolk

British Library Cataloguing in Publication Data
A catalogue record for this book is available from the British Library

ISBN 978-0–415–27836–2 (hbk)
ISBN 978-0–415–27837–9 (pbk)

CONTENTS

ACKNOWLEDGEMENTS

Grateful acknowledgement is here made to Miss Barbara Hannah, for carefully checking the typescript of this translation; to Mr. A. S. B. Glover, for compiling the Index; and to Amherst Press, California, for permission to quote from *The Secret of the Saucers*, by Orfeo M. Angelucci.

PLATES

Figures

PREFACE TO THE ENGLISH EDITION

The worldwide rumour about Flying Saucers presents a problem that challenges the psychologist for a number of reasons. The primary question—and apparently this is the most important point—is this: are they real or are they mere fantasy products? This question is by no means settled yet. If they are real, exactly what are they? If they are fantasy, why should such a rumour exist?

In this latter respect I have made an interesting and quite unexpected discovery. In 1954 I gave an interview to the Swiss weekly, Die Weltwoche, in which I expressed myself in a sceptical way, though I spoke with due respect of the serious opinion of a relatively large number of air specialists who believe in the reality of UFOs (unidentified flying objects). In 1958 this interview was suddenly discovered by the world press and the "news" spread like wildfire from the far West round the earth to the far East, but—alas—in distorted form. I was quoted as a saucer-believer. I issued a statement to the United Press and gave a true version of my opinion, but this time the wire went dead:

nobody, so far as I know, took any notice of it, except one German newspaper.

The moral of this story is rather interesting. As the behaviour of the press is a sort of Gallup test with reference to world opinion, one must draw the conclusion that news affirming the existence of UFOs is welcome, but that scepticism seems to be undesirable. To believe that UFOs are real suits the general opinion, whereas disbelief is to be discouraged. This creates the impression that there is a tendency all over the world to believe in saucers and to want them to be real, unconsciously helped along by a press that otherwise has no sympathy with the phenomenon.

This remarkable fact in itself surely merits the psychologist's interest. Why should it be more desirable for saucers to exist than not? The following pages are an attempt to answer this question. I have relieved the text of cumbersome footnotes, except for a few which give the references for the interested reader.

C. G. JUNG

September, 1958

INTRODUCTORY

It is difficult to form a correct estimate of the significance of contemporary events, and the danger that our judgment will remain caught in subjectivity is great. So I am fully aware of the risk I am taking in proposing to communicate my views concerning certain contemporary events, which seem to me important, to those who are patient enough to hear me. I refer to those reports reaching us from all corners of the earth, rumours of round objects that flash through the troposphere and stratosphere, and go by the name of Flying Saucers, *soucoupes*, disks, and "UFOs" (Unidentified Flying Objects). These rumours, or the possible physical existence of such objects, seem to me so significant that I feel myself compelled, as once before[1] when events were brewing of fateful consequence for Europe, to sound a note of warning. I know that, just as before, my voice is much too weak to reach the ear of the multitude. It is not presumption

---

[1] "Wotan", *Essays on Contemporary Events*, London, 1947; first published in the *Neue Schweizer Rundschau*, 1936.

that drives me, but my conscience as a psychiatrist that bids me fulfil my duty and prepare those few who will hear me for coming events which are in accord with the end of an era. As we know from ancient Egyptian history, they are symptoms of psychic changes that always appear at the end of one Platonic month and at the beginning of another. They are, it seems, changes in the constellation of psychic dominants, of the archetypes, or "gods" as they used to be called, which bring about, or accompany, long-lasting transformations of the collective psyche. This transformation started within the historical tradition and left traces behind it, first in the transition from the age of Taurus to that of Aries, and then from Aries to Pisces, whose beginning coincides with the rise of Christianity. We are now nearing that great change which may be expected when the spring-point enters Aquarius. It would be frivolous of me to conceal from the reader that reflections such as these are not only exceedingly unpopular but come perilously close to those turbid fantasies which becloud the minds of world-improvers and other interpreters of "signs and portents". But I must take this risk, even if it means putting my hard-won reputation for truthfulness, trustworthiness, and scientific judgment in jeopardy. I can assure my readers that I do not do this with a light heart. I am, to be quite frank, concerned for all those who are caught unprepared by the events in question and disconcerted by their incomprehensible nature. Since, so far as I know, no one has yet felt moved to examine and set forth the possible psychic consequences of this foreseeable change, I deem it my duty to do what I can in this respect. I undertake this thankless task in the expectation that my chisel will make no impression on the hard stone it meets.

Some time ago I wrote a short article in which I considered the nature of "Flying Saucers".[2] I came to the same conclusion as the semi-official report by Edward I. Ruppelt, one-time chief of

---

[2] "Weltwoche", 22. Jahrg., Nr. 1078, July 1954.

the American Bureau for observing UFOs.[3] The conclusion is: *something is seen, but one doesn't know what.* It is difficult, if not impossible, to form any correct idea of these objects, because they behave not like bodies but like weightless thoughts. Up till now there has been no indisputable proof of the physical existence of UFOs except for the cases picked up by radar. I have discussed the reliability of these radar observations with Prof. Max Knoll, a specialist in this field. What he says is not encouraging. Nevertheless, there do seem to be authenticated cases where the visual observation was confirmed by a radar echo. I would like to call the reader's attention to Keyhoe's books, which are based on official material and studiously avoid the wild speculation, naïveté or prejudice of other publications.[4]

For a decade the physical reality of UFOs remained a very problematical matter, which was not decided one way or the other with the necessary clarity, despite the mass of observational material that had accumulated in the meantime. The longer the uncertainty lasted, the greater became the probability that this obviously complicated phenomenon had an extremely important psychic component as well as a possible physical basis. This is not surprising, in that we are dealing with an ostensibly physical phenomenon distinguished on the one hand by its frequent appearances, and on the other by its strange, unknown, and indeed contradictory nature.

Such an object provokes, like nothing else, conscious and unconscious fantasies, the former giving rise to speculative conjectures and pure fabrications, and the latter supplying the mythological background inseparable from these provocative observations. Thus there arose a situation in which, with the best

[3] *The Report on Unidentified Flying Objects*, New York, 1956.
[4] Major Donald E. Keyhoe, *Flying Saucers from Outer Space*, New York, 1953, and *The Flying Saucer Conspiracy*, London, 1957. Cf. also Aimé Michel, *The Truth about Saucers*, London, 1957.

will in the world, one often did not know and could not discover whether a primary perception was followed by a phantasm or whether, conversely, a primary fantasy originating in the unconscious invaded the conscious mind with illusions and visions. The material that has become known to me during the past ten years lends support to both hypotheses. In the first case an objectively real, physical process forms the basis for an accompanying myth; in the second case an archetype creates the corresponding vision. To these two causal relationships we must add a third possibility, namely, that of a "synchronistic", i.e., acausal, meaningful coincidence—a problem that has occupied men's minds ever since the time of Geulincx, Leibniz, and Schopenhauer.[5] It is a hypothesis that has special bearing on phenomena connected with archetypal psychic processes.

As a psychologist, I am not qualified to contribute anything useful to the question of the physical reality of UFOs. I can concern myself only with their undoubted psychic aspect, and in what follows shall deal almost exclusively with their psychic concomitants.

---

[5] Cf. my paper "Synchronicity: An Acausal Connecting Principle", Jung and Pauli, *The Interpretation of Nature and the Psyche*, London and New York, 1955.

1

UFOS AS RUMOURS

Since the things reported of UFOs not only sound incredible but seem to fly in the face of all our basic assumptions about the physical world, it is very natural that one's first reaction should be the negative one of outright rejection. Surely, we say, it's nothing but illusions, fantasies, and lies. People who report such stuff—chiefly airline pilots and ground staff—cannot be quite right in the head! What is worse, most of these stories come from America, the land of superlatives and of science fiction.

In order to meet this natural reaction, we shall begin by considering the UFO reports simply as rumours, i.e., as psychic products, and shall draw from this all the conclusions that are warranted by an analytical method of procedure.

Regarded in this light, the UFO reports may seem to the sceptical mind to be rather like a story that is told all over the world, but differs from an ordinary rumour in that it is expressed in the form of visions,[1] or perhaps owed its existence to them in the

---

[1] I prefer the term "vision" to "hallucination", because the latter bears the stamp of a pathological concept, whereas a vision is a phenomenon that is by no means peculiar to pathological states.

first place and is now kept alive by them. I would call this comparatively rare variation a *visionary rumour*. It is closely akin to the collective visions of, say, the crusaders during the siege of Jerusalem, the troops at Mons in the first World War, the faithful followers of the Pope at Fatima, Portugal, etc. Apart from collective visions, there are on record cases where one or more persons see something that physically is not there. For instance, I was once at a spiritualistic séance where four of the five people present saw a object like a moon floating above the abdomen of the medium. They showed me, the fifth person present, exactly where it was, and it was absolutely incomprehensible to them that I could see nothing of the sort. I know of three more cases where certain objects were seen in the clearest detail (in two of them by two persons, and in the third by one person) and could afterwards be proved to be non-existent. Two of these cases happened under my direct observation. Even people who are entirely *compos mentis* and in full possession of their senses can sometimes see things that do not exist. I do not know what the explanation is of such happenings. It is very possible that they are less rare than I am inclined to suppose. For as a rule we do not verify things we have "seen with our own eyes", and so we never get to know that actually they did not exist. I mention these somewhat remote possibilities because, in such an unusual matter as the UFOs, one has to take every aspect into account.

The first requisite for a visionary rumour, as distinct from an ordinary rumour, for whose dissemination nothing more is needed than popular curiosity and sensation-mongering, is always an *unusual emotion*. Its intensification into a vision and delusion of the senses, however, springs from a stronger excitation and therefore from a deeper source.

The signal for the UFO stories was given by the mysterious projectiles seen over Sweden during the last two years of the war—attributed of course to the Russians—and by the reports about "Foo fighters", i.e. lights that accompanied the Allied bombers over Germany (Foo=feu). These were followed by the strange sightings of "Flying Saucers" in America. The impossibility of finding an earthly base for the UFOs and of explaining their physical peculiarities soon led to the conjecture of an extra-terrestrial origin. With this development the rumour got linked up with the psychology of the great panic that broke out in New Jersey just before the second World War, when a radio play, based on a novel by H. G. Wells, about Martians invading New York, caused a regular stampede with numerous car accidents. The play evidently hit the latent emotion connected with the imminence of war.

The motif of an extra-terrestrial invasion was seized upon by the rumour and the UFOs were interpreted as machines controlled by intelligent beings from outer space. The apparently weightless behaviour of space-ships and their intelligent, purposive movements were attributed to the superior technical knowledge and ability of the cosmic intruders. As they did no harm and refrained from all hostile acts it was assumed that their appearance over the earth was due to curiosity or to the need for aerial reconnaissance. It also seemed that airfields and atomic installations in particular held a special attraction for them, from which it was concluded that the dangerous development of atomic physics and nuclear fission had caused a certain disquiet on our neighbouring planets and necessitated a more accurate survey from the air. As a result, people felt they were being observed and spied upon from space.

The rumour actually gained so much official recognition that Service Chiefs in America set up a special bureau for collecting, analyzing, and evaluating all relevant observations. This seems to have been done also in France, Italy, Sweden, Great Britain, and other countries. After the publication of Ruppelt's report the Saucer stories seem to have more or less vanished from the press for about a year. They were evidently no longer "news".

That the interest in UFOs and, probably, the sightings of them have not ceased is shown by the recent press report that an American admiral has suggested that clubs be founded all over the country for collecting UFO reports and investigating them in detail.

The rumour states that the UFOs are as a rule lens-shaped, but can also be oblong or shaped like cigars; that they shine in various colours or have a metallic glitter;[2] that from a stationary position they can attain a speed of about 10,000 miles per hour, and that at times their acceleration is such that if anything resembling a human being were to guide it he would be instantly killed. In flight they turn off at angles that would be possible only to a weightless object.

Their flight, accordingly, resembles that of a flying insect. Like this, the UFO can suddenly hover over an interesting object for quite a time, or circle round it inquisitively, just as suddenly to dart off again and discover new objects in its zigzag flight. UFOs are therefore not to be confused with meteorites or with reflections from so-called "temperature inversion layers". Their alleged interest in airfields and in industrial installations connected with nuclear fission is not always confirmed, since they are also seen in the Antarctic, in the Sahara, and in the Himalayas. For preference, however, they seem to swarm over the United States, though recent reports show that they do a good deal of flying over the Old World and in the Far East. Nobody knows what they are looking for or what they want to observe. Our aeroplanes seem to arouse their curiosity, for they often fly towards them or pursue them. But they also fly away from them. Their flights do not appear to be based on any recognizable system. They behave more like groups of tourists unsystematically viewing the countryside, pausing now here for a while and

---

[2] Special emphasis should be laid on the *green* fire-balls frequently observed in the south-west of the USA.

now there, erratically following first one interest and then
another, sometimes shooting to enormous altitudes for inexplicable reasons or performing acrobatic evolutions before
the noses of exasperated pilots. Sometimes they appear to be up
to 500 yards in diameter, sometimes small as electric street-
lamps. There are large motherships from which little UFOs slip
out or in which they take shelter. They are said to be both
manned and unmanned, and in the latter case are remote-
controlled. According to the rumour, the occupants are about
three feet high and look like human beings, or, conversely, are
utterly unlike us. Other reports speak of giants fifteen feet high.
They are beings who are carrying out a cautious survey of the
earth and considerately avoid all encounters with men, or,
more menacingly, are spying out landing places with a view to
settling the population of a planet that has got into difficulties
and colonizing the earth by force. Uncertainty in regard to the
physical conditions on earth and their fear of unknown sources
of infection have held them back temporarily from drastic
encounters and even from attempted landings, although they
possess frightful weapons which would enable them to
exterminate the human race. In addition to their obviously
superior technology they are credited with superior wisdom
and moral goodness which would, on the other hand, enable
them to save humanity. Naturally there are stories of landings,
too, when the saucer-men were not only seen at close quarters
but attempted to carry off a human being. Even a reliable man
like Keyhoe gives us to understand that a squadron of five
military aircraft plus a large sea plane were swallowed up by
UFO motherships in the vicinity of the Bahamas, and carried
off.

One's hair stands on end when one reads such reports
together with the documentary evidence. And when one considers the known possibility of tracking UFOs with radar, then we
have all the essentials for an unsurpassable "science fiction

story". Every man who prides himself on his sound common sense will feel distinctly affronted. I shall therefore not enter here into the various attempts at explanation to which the rumour has given rise.

While I was engaged in writing this essay, it so happened that two articles appeared more or less simultaneously in leading American newspapers, showing very clearly how the problem stands at present. The first was a report on the latest UFO sighting by a pilot who was flying an aircraft to Puerto Rico with forty-four passengers. While he was over the ocean he saw a "fiery, round object, shining with greenish white light", coming towards him at great speed. At first he thought it was a jet-propelled aircraft, but soon saw that it was some unusual and unknown object. In order to avoid collision, he pulled his aircraft into such a steep climb that the passengers were shot out of their seats and tumbled over one another. Four of them received injuries requiring hospital attention. Seven other aircraft strung out along the same route of about 300 miles sighted the same object.

The other article, entitled "No Flying Saucers, U.S. Expert Says", concerns the categorical statement made by Dr. Hugh L. Dryden, director of the National Advisory Committee for Aeronautics, that UFOs do not exist. One cannot but respect the unflinching scepticism of Dr. Dryden; it gives stout-hearted expression to the feeling that such preposterous rumours are an offence to human dignity.

If we close our eyes a little so as to overlook certain details, it is possible to side with the reasonable opinion of the majority in whose name Dr. Dryden speaks, and to regard the thousands of UFO reports and the uproar they have created as a visionary rumour, to be treated accordingly. They would then boil down, objectively, to an admittedly impressive collection of mistaken observations and conclusions into which subjective psychic assumptions have been projected.

But if it is a case of psychological *projection*, there must be a *psychic cause* for it. One can hardly suppose that anything of such worldwide incidence as the UFO legend is purely fortuitous and of no importance whatever. The many thousands of individual testimonies must have an equally extensive causal basis. When an assertion of this kind is corroborated practically everywhere, we are driven to assume that a corresponding motive must be present everywhere, too. Though visionary rumours may be caused or accompanied by all manner of outward circumstances, they are based essentially on an omnipresent emotional foundation, in this case a psychological situation common to all mankind. The basis for this kind of rumour is an *emotional tension* having its cause in a situation of collective distress or danger, or in a vital psychic need. This condition undoubtedly exists today, in so far as the whole world is suffering under the strain of Russian policies and their still unpredictable consequences. In the individual, too, such phenomena as abnormal convictions, visions, illusions, etc., only occur when he is suffering from a psychic dissociation, that is, when there is a split between the conscious attitude and the unconscious contents opposed to it. Precisely because the conscious mind does not know about them and is therefore confronted with a situation from which there seems to be no way out, these strange contents cannot be integrated directly but seek to express themselves indirectly, thus giving rise to unexpected and apparently inexplicable opinions, beliefs, illusions, visions, and so forth. Any unusual natural occurrences such as meteors, comets, "rains of blood", a calf with two heads, and suchlike abortions are interpreted as menacing omens, or else signs are seen in the heavens. Things can be seen by many people independently of one another, or even simultaneously, which are not physically real. Also, the association processes of many people often have a parallelism in time and space, with the result that different people, simultaneously and independently of one another, can produce the same new ideas, as has happened numerous times in history.

In addition, there are cases where the same collective cause produces identical or similar effects, i.e., the same visionary images and interpretations in the very people who are least prepared for such phenomena and least inclined to believe in them.[3] This fact gives the eyewitness accounts an air of particular credibility: it is usually emphasized that the witness is above suspicion because he was never distinguished for his lively imagination or credulousness but, on the contrary, for his cool judgment and critical reason. In just these cases the unconscious has to resort to particularly drastic measures in order to make its contents perceived. It does this most vividly by projection, by extrapolating its contents into an object, which then mirrors what had previously lain hidden in the unconscious. Projection can be observed at work everywhere, in mental illnesses, ideas of persecution and hallucinations, in so-called normal people who see the mote in their brother's eye without seeing the beam in their own, and finally, in extreme form, in political propaganda.

Projections have what we might call different ranges, according to whether they stem from merely personal conditions or from deeper collective ones. Personal repressions and things of which we are unconscious manifest themselves in our immediate environment, in our circle of relatives and acquaintances. Collective contents, such as religious, philosophical, political and social conflicts, select projection-carriers of a corresponding kind—Freemasons, Jesuits, Jews, Capitalists, Bolsheviks, Imperialists, etc. In the threatening situation of the world today, when people are beginning to see that everything is at stake, the projection-creating fantasy soars beyond the realm of earthly organizations and powers into the heavens, into interstellar

---

[3] Aimé Michel remarks that UFOs are mostly seen by people who do not believe in them or who regard the whole problem with indifference.

space, where the rulers of human fate, the gods, once had their abode in the planets. Our earthly world is split into two halves, and nobody knows where a helpful solution is to come from. Even people who would never have thought that a religious problem could be a serious matter that concerned them personally are beginning to ask themselves fundamental questions. Under these circumstances it would not be at all surprising if those sections of the community who ask themselves nothing were visited by "visions", that is, by a widespread myth seriously believed in by some and rejected as absurd by others. Eye-witnesses of unimpeachable honesty therefore announce the "signs in the heavens" which they have seen "with their own eyes", and the marvellous things they have experienced which pass human understanding.

All these reports have naturally resulted in a clamorous demand for explanation. Initial attempts to explain the UFOs as Russian or American inventions soon came to grief on their apparently weightless behaviour, which is unknown to earth-dwellers. Human fantasy, already toying with the idea of space-trips to the moon, therefore had no hesitation in assuming that intelligent beings of a higher order had learnt how to counteract gravitation and, by dint of using interstellar magnetic fields as sources of power, to travel through space with the speed of light. The recent atomic explosions on the earth, it was conjectured, had aroused the attention of these so very much more advanced dwellers on Mars or Venus, who were worried about possible chain-reactions and the consequent destruction of our planet. Since such a possibility would constitute a catastrophic threat to our neighbouring planets, their inhabitants felt compelled to observe how things were developing on earth, fully aware of the tremendous cataclysm our clumsy nuclear experiments might unleash. The fact that the UFOs neither land on earth nor show the least inclination to get into communication with human beings is met by the explanation that these visitors, despite their superior knowledge, are not at all certain of being well received on earth, for which reason they carefully avoid all intelligent contact with humans. But because they, as befitted superior beings, conduct themselves quite inoffensively, they would do the earth no harm and are satisfied with an objective inspection of airfields and atomic installations. Just why these higher beings, who show such a burning interest in the fate of the earth, have still not found some way of communicating with us after ten years—despite their knowledge of languages—remains shrouded in darkness. Other explanations have therefore to be sought, for instance that a planet has got into difficulties, perhaps through the drying up of its water supplies, or loss of oxygen, or overpopulation, and is looking for a *pied-à-terre*. The reconnaissance patrols are going to work with the utmost care and circumspection, despite the fact that they have been giving a benefit performance in the heavens for hundreds, if not thousands, of years. Since the Second World War they have appeared in masses, obviously because an imminent landing is planned. Recently their harmlessness has been doubted. There are also stories by so-called eyewitnesses who declare they have seen UFOs landing with, of course, English-speaking occupants. These space-guests are sometimes idealized figures along the lines of technological angels who are concerned for our welfare, sometimes dwarfs with enormous heads bursting with intelligence, sometimes lemur-like creatures covered with hair and equipped with claws, or dwarfish monsters clad in armour and looking like insects.

There are even "eyewitnesses" like Mr. Adamski, who relates that he has flown in a UFO and made a round trip of the moon in a few hours. He brings us the astonishing news that the side of the moon turned away from us contains atmosphere, water, forests, and settlements, without being in the least perturbed by the moon's skittishness in turning just her unhospitable side towards the earth. This physical monstrosity of a story was actually swallowed by a cultivated and well-meaning person like Edgar Sievers.[4]

Considering the notorious camera-mindedness of Americans, it is surprising how few "authentic" photos of UFOs seem to exist, especially as many of them are said to have been observed for several hours at relatively close quarters. I myself happen to know someone who saw a UFO with hundreds of other people in Guatemala. He had his camera with him, but in the excitement he completely forgot to take a photo, although it was daytime and the UFO remained visible for an hour. I have no reason to doubt the honesty of his report. He has merely strengthened my impression that UFOs are somehow not photogenic.

As one can see from all this the observation and interpretation of UFOs has already led to the formation of a regular legend. Quite apart from the thousands of newspaper reports and articles there is now a whole literature on the subject, some of it humbug, some of it serious. The UFOs themselves, however, do not appear to have been impressed; as the latest observations show, they continue their way undeterred. Be that as it may, one thing is certain: they have become a living myth. We have here a golden opportunity to see how a legend is formed, and how in a difficult and dark time for humanity a miraculous tale grows up of an attempted intervention by extra-terrestrial "heavenly" powers—and this at the very time when human fantasy is seriously considering the possibility of space travel and of visiting or even invading other planets. We on our side want to fly to the moon or to Mars, and on their side the inhabitants of other planets in our system, or even of the fixed stars, want to fly to us. We at least are conscious of our space-conquering aspirations, but that a corresponding extra-terrestrial tendency exists is a purely mythological conjecture, i.e., a projection.

Sensationalism, love of adventure, technological audacity,

----

[4] Cf. *Flying Saucers über Südafrika*, Pretoria, 1955.

intellectual curiosity may appear to be sufficient motives for our futuristic fantasies, but the impulse to spin such fantasies, especially when they take such a serious form—witness the sputniks—springs from an underlying cause, namely a situation of distress and the vital need that goes with it. It could easily be conjectured that the earth is growing too small for us, that humanity would like to escape from its prison, where we are threatened not only by the hydrogen bomb but, at a still deeper level, by the prodigious increase in the population figures, which give cause for serious concern. This is a problem which people do not like to talk about, or then only with optimistic references to the incalculable possibilities of intensive food production, as if this were anything more than a postponement of the final solution. As a precautionary measure the Indian government has granted half a million pounds for birth control propaganda, while the Russians exploit the labour-camp system as one way of skimming off the dreaded excess of births. Though the highly civilized countries of the West know how to help themselves in other ways, the immediate danger does not come from them but from the underdeveloped peoples of Asia and Africa. This is not the place to discuss the question of how far the two World Wars were an outlet for this pressing problem of keeping down the population at all costs. Nature has many ways of disposing of her surplus.

Man's living space is, in fact, continually shrinking and for many races the optimum has long been exceeded. The danger of catastrophe grows in proportion as the expanding populations impinge on one another. Congestion creates fear, which looks for help from extra-terrestrial sources since it cannot be found on earth.

Hence there appear "signs in the heavens", superior beings in the kind of space ships devised by our technological fantasy. From a fear whose cause is far from being fully understood and is therefore not conscious, there arise explanatory projections which purport to find the cause in all manner of secondary phenomena, however unsuitable. Some of these projections are so obvious that it seems almost superfluous to dig any deeper.[5] But if we want to understand a mass rumour which, it appears, is even accompanied by collective visions, we must not remain satisfied with all too rational and superficially obvious motives. The cause must strike at the roots of our existence if it is to explain such an extraordinary phenomenon as the UFOs. Although they were observed as rare curiosities in earlier centuries, they merely gave rise to the usual local rumours.

The universal mass rumour was reserved for our enlightened, rationalistic age. The widespread fantasy about the destruction of the world at the end of the first millennium was metaphysical in origin and needed no UFOs in order to appear rational. Heaven's intervention was quite consistent with the *Weltanschauung* of the age. But nowadays public opinion would hardly be inclined to resort to the hypothesis of a metaphysical act, otherwise innumerable parsons would already have been preaching about the warning signs in heaven. Our *Weltanschauung* does not expect anything of this sort. We would be much more inclined to think of the possibility of *psychic* disturbances and interventions, especially as our psychic equilibrium has become something of a problem since the last World War. In this respect there is increasing uncertainty. Even our historians can no longer make use of the conventional techniques in evaluating and explaining the developments that have overtaken Europe in the last few decades, but must admit that psychological and psychopathological factors are beginning to widen the horizons of historiography in an alarming way. The growing interest which the thinking public consequently evinces in psychology has already aroused the displeasure of the academies and of incompetent specialists. In spite

[5] Cf. Eugen Böhler's enlightening remarks in *Ethik und Wirtschaft* (Industrielle Organization, Zürich, 1957).

of the palpable resistance to psychology emanating from these circles, psychologists who are conscious of their responsibilities should not be dissuaded from critically examining a mass phenomenon like the UFOs, since the apparent impossibility of the reports suggests to common sense that the most likely explanation lies in a psychic disturbance.

We shall therefore turn our attention to the psychic aspect of the phenomenon. For this purpose we shall briefly review the central statements of the rumour: certain objects are seen in the earth's atmosphere, both by day and by night, which are unlike any known meteorological phenomena. They are not meteors, not misidentified fixed stars, not "temperature inversions", not cloud formations, not migrating birds, not aerial balloons, not balls of fire, and certainly not the delirious products of intoxication or fever, nor the plain lies of eyewitnesses. What as a rule is seen is a body of round shape, disk-like or spherical, glowing or shining fierily in different colours, or, more seldom, a cigar-shaped or cylindrical figure of various sizes.[6] It is reported that occasionally they are invisible to the naked eye but leave a "blip" on the radar screen. The round bodies in particular are figures such as the unconscious produces in dreams, visions, etc. In the latter case they are to be regarded as *symbols* representing, in visual form, some thought that was not thought consciously, but is merely potentially present in the unconscious, in invisible form, and attains visibility only through the process of becoming conscious. The visible form, however, expresses the meaning of the unconscious content only approximately. In practice the meaning has to be completed by amplificatory interpretation. The unavoidable errors that result can be eliminated only

---

[6] The more rarely reported cigar form may have the Zeppelin for a model. The obvious phallic comparison, i.e. the translation into sexual language, springs naturally to the lips of the people. Berliners, for instance, refer to the cigar-shaped UFO as a "holy ghost", and the Swiss military have an even more outspoken name for observation balloons.

through the principle of "waiting on events"; that is to say we obtain a consistent and readable text by comparing sequences of dreams dreamt by different individuals. The figures in a rumour can be subjected to the same principles of dream interpretation.

If we apply them to the round object—whether it be a disk or a sphere—we at once get an analogy with the symbol of totality well-known to all students of depth psychology, namely the *mandala* (Sanskrit for circle). This is not by any means a new invention, for it can be found in all epochs and in all places, always with the same meaning, and reappears time and again, independently of tradition, in modern individuals as the "protective" or apotropaic circle, whether in the form of the prehistoric "sun wheel", or the magic circle, or the alchemical microcosm, or a modern *symbol of order*, which organizes and encloses the psychic totality. As I have shown elsewhere,[7] in the course of the centuries the mandala has developed into a definitely psychological totality symbol, as the history of alchemy proves. I would like to show how the mandala appears in a modern person by citing the dream of a 6-year-old girl:

> She dreamt she stood at the entrance of a large, unknown building. There a fairy was waiting for her, who led her inside, into a long colonnade, and conducted her to a sort of central chamber, with similar colonnades converging from all sides. The fairy stepped into the centre and changed herself into a tall flame. Three snakes crawled round the fire, as if circumambulating it.

Here we have a classic, archetypal childhood dream such as is not only dreamt fairly often but is sometimes drawn or painted, without any suggestion from outside, for the evident purpose of

---

[7] "On Mandala Symbolism", Coll. Works, vol. 9, Part I.

warding off disagreeable or disturbing family influences and preserving the inner balance.

In so far as the mandala encompasses, protects, and defends the psychic totality against outside influences and seeks to unite the inner opposites, it is at the same time a distinct *individuation symbol* and was known as such even to medieval alchemy. The soul was supposed to have the form of a sphere, on the analogy of Plato's world-soul, and we meet the same symbol in modern dreams. By reason of its antiquity, this symbol leads us to the heavenly spheres, to Plato's "supra-celestial place", where the "Ideas" of all things are stored up. Hence there would be nothing against the naïve interpretation of the UFOs as "souls". Naturally they do not represent our modern conception of the soul, but rather an involuntary archetypal or mythological conception of an unconscious content, a *rotundum*, as the alchemists called it, that expresses the totality of the individual. I have defined this spontaneous image as a symbolical representation of the *self*, by which I mean not the ego but the totality composed of the conscious *and* the unconscious.[8] I am not alone in this, as the Hermetic philosophy of the Middle Ages had already arrived at very similar conclusions. The archetypal character of this idea is borne out by its spontaneous recurrence in modern individuals who know nothing of any such tradition, any more than those around them. Even people who might know of it never imagine that their children could dream of anything so remote as Hermetic philosophy. In this matter the deepest and darkest ignorance prevails, which is of course the most unsuitable vehicle for mythological tradition.

If the round shining objects that appear in the sky be regarded as visions, we can hardly avoid interpreting them as archetypal images. They would then be involuntary, automatic projections based on instinct, and as little as any other psychic

[8] Cf. "The Self", ibid., Part II.

manifestations or symptoms can they be dismissed as meaning-less and merely fortuitous. Anyone with the requisite historical and psychological knowledge knows that circular symbols have played an important role in every age; in our own sphere of culture, for instance, they were not only soul symbols but "God-images". There is an old saying that "God is a circle whose centre is everywhere and the circumference nowhere". God in his omniscience, omnipotence, and omnipresence is a totality sym-bol *par excellence*, something round, complete, and perfect. Epiph-anies of this sort are, in the tradition, often associated with fire and light. On the antique level, therefore, the UFOs could easily be conceived as "gods". They are impressive manifest-ations of totality whose simple, round form portrays the archetype of the self, which as we know from experience plays the chief role in uniting apparently irreconcilable opposites and is therefore best suited to compensate the split-mindedness of our age. It has a particularly important role to play among the other archetypes in that it is primarily the regulator and orderer of chaotic states, giving the personality the greatest possible unity and wholeness. It creates the image of the divine-human personality, the Primordial Man or Anthropos, a *chen-yen* (true or whole man), an Elijah who calls down fire from heaven, rises up to heaven in a fiery char-iot,[9] and is a forerunner of the Messiah, the dogmatized figure of Christ, as well as of Khidr, the Verdant One,[10] who is another parallel to Elijah: like him, he wanders over the earth as a human personification of Allah.

The present world situation is calculated as never before to arouse expectations of a redeeming, supernatural event. If these expectations have not dared to show themselves very clearly, this is simply because no one is deeply rooted enough in the

---

[9] Significantly enough, Elijah also appears as an eagle, who spies out unrighteousness on earth from above.

[10] Cf. "Concerning Rebirth", Coll. Works, vol. 9, Part I.

tradition of earlier centuries to consider an intervention from heaven as a matter of course. We have indeed strayed far from the metaphysical certainties of the Middle Ages, but not so far that our historical and psychological background is empty of all metaphysical hope.[11] Consciously, however, rationalistic enlightenment predominates, and this abhors all leanings towards the "occult". Desperate efforts are made for a "repristination" of our Christian faith, but we cannot get back to that limited world view which in former times left room for metaphysical intervention. Nor can we resuscitate a genuine Christian belief in an after-life or the equally Christian hope for an imminent end of the world that would put a definite stop to the regrettable error of Creation. Belief in this world and in the power of man has, despite assurances to the contrary, become a practical and, for the time being, irrefragable truth.

This attitude on the part of the overwhelming majority provides the most favourable basis for a projection, that is, for a manifestation of the unconscious background. Undeterred by rationalistic criticism, it thrusts itself to the forefront in the form of a symbolic rumour, accompanied and reinforced by the appropriate visions, and in so doing activates an archetype that has always expressed order, deliverance, salvation, and wholeness. It is characteristic of our time that, in contrast to its previous expressions, the archetype should now take the form of an object, a technological construction, in order to avoid the odiousness of a mythological personification. Anything that looks technological goes down without difficulty with modern man. The possibility of space travel makes the unpopular idea of a metaphysical intervention much more acceptable. The apparent

[11] It is a common and totally unjustified misunderstanding on the part of scientifically trained people to say that I regard the psychic background as something "metaphysical", while on the other hand the theologians accuse me of "psychologizing" metaphysics. Both are wide of the mark: I am an empiricist, who keeps within the boundaries set for him by the theory of knowledge.

weightlessness of the UFOs, is, of course, rather hard to digest, but then our own physicists have discovered so many things that border on the miraculous: why should not more advanced star-dwellers have discovered a way to counteract gravitation and reach the speed of light, if not more?

Nuclear physics has begotten in the layman's head an uncertainty of judgment that far exceeds that of the physicists, and makes things appear possible which but a short while ago would have been declared nonsensical. Consequently the UFOs can easily be regarded and believed in as a physicists' miracle. I still remember, with misgivings, the time when I was convinced that something heavier than air could not fly, only to be taught a painful lesson. Nevertheless, the apparently physical nature of the UFOs creates such insoluble puzzles for even the best brains, and on the other hand has built up such an impressive legend, that one feels tempted to take them as a 99 per cent psychic product and subject them accordingly to the usual psychological interpretation. Should it be that an unknown physical phe- nomenon is the outward cause of the myth, this would detract nothing from the myth, for many myths have meteorological and other natural phenomena as accompanying causes which by no means explain them. A myth is essentially a product of the unconscious archetype and is therefore a symbol which requires psychological interpretation. For primitive man any object, for instance an old tin that has been thrown away, can suddenly assume the importance of a fetish. This effect is obviously not inherent in the tin, but is a psychic product.

2

UFOS IN DREAMS

Not only are UFOs seen, they are of course also dreamt about. This is particularly interesting to the psychologist, because the dreams tell us in what sense they are understood by the unconscious. In order to form anything like a complete picture of an object reflected in the psyche, far more than an exclusively intellectual operation is required. In addition to the three other functions of feeling (valuation), sensation (reality-sense), and intuition (perception of possibilities), we need the reaction of the unconscious, i.e., the picture of the unconscious associative context. It is this total view that alone makes possible a whole judgment on the psychic situation constellated by the object. An exclusively intellectual approach is bound to be from 50 to 75 per cent unsatisfactory.

By way of illustration I shall cite two dreams dreamt by an educated lady. She had never seen a UFO, but was interested in the phenomenon without being able to form a definite picture of it. She did not know the UFO literature, nor was she acquainted with my ideas on the subject.

DREAM 1

I was going down the Champs Elysées in a bus, with many other people. Suddenly the air-raid warning sounded. The bus stopped and all the passengers jumped out, and the next moment they had disappeared into the nearest houses, banging the doors behind them. I was the last to leave the bus. I tried to get into a house, but all the doors with their polished brass knobs were tightly shut, and the whole Champs Elysées was empty. I pressed against the wall of a house and looked up at the sky: instead of the expected bombers I saw a sort of Flying Saucer, a metallic sphere shaped like a drop. It was flying along quite slowly from north to east, and I had the impression that I was being observed. In the silence I heard the high heels of a woman who was walking alone on the empty sidewalk down the Champs Elysées. The atmosphere was most uncanny.

DREAM 2 (ABOUT A MONTH LATER)

I was walking, at night, in the streets of a city. Interplanetary "machines" appeared in the sky, and everyone fled. The "machines" looked like large steel cigars. I did not flee. One of the "machines" spotted me and came straight towards me at an oblique angle. I think: Professor Jung says that one should not run away, so I stand still and look at the machine. From the front, seen close to, it looked like a circular eye, half blue, half white.

A room in a hospital: my two chiefs come in, very worried, and ask my sister how it is going. My sister replied that the mere sight of the machine had burnt my whole face. Only then did I realize that they were talking about me, and that my whole head was bandaged, although I could not see it.

COMMENTARY TO DREAM 1

The dream describes, as the exposition of the initial situation, a mass panic as at an air-raid warning. A UFO appears, having the form of a drop. A fluid body assumes the form of a drop when it is about to fall, from which it is clear that the UFO is conceived as a liquid falling from the sky, like rain. This surprising drop-form of the UFO and the analogy with a fluid occur in the literature.[1] Presumably it is meant to express the commonly reported changeability of the UFO's shape. This "heavenly" fluid must be of a mysterious nature and is probably a conception similar to that of the alchemical *aqua permanens*, the "permanent water", which was also called "Heaven" in sixteenth-century alchemy and stood for the *quinta essentia*. This water is the *deus ex machina* of alchemy, the wonderful solvent, the word *solutio* being used equally for a chemical solution and for the solution of a problem. Indeed, it is the great magician Mercurius himself, the dissolver and binder ("solve et coagula"), the physical and spiritual panacea, which at the same time can be something threatening and dangerous, and falls as the *aqua coelestis* from heaven.

Just as the alchemists speak of their "stone, which is no stone", so also of their "philosophical" water, which is no water, but quicksilver, and no ordinary Hg at that, but a "spirit" (pneuma). It represents the arcane substance, which during the alchemical operations changes from a base metal into a spiritual form, often personified as the *filius hermaphroditus*, *filius Macrocosmi*, etc. The "water of the Philosophers" is the classic substance that transmutes the chemical elements and during their transformation is itself transformed. It is also the "redeeming spirit". These ideas began far back in the literature of antiquity, underwent further development during the Middle Ages, and even

[1] A report on the case of Captain Mantell, now become a classic, speaks of the UFO's resemblance to a "tear drop", and says it behaved like a fluid. Cf. Harold T. Wilkins, *Flying Saucers on the Moon*, London (no date), p. 90.

penetrated into folk-lore and fairy-tale. A very ancient text (possibly first century A.D.) says that in the stone that is found in the Nile there is a spirit. "Reach in thy hand and draw forth the spirit. That is the *exhydrargyrosis* (the expulsion of the quicksilver)". For a period of nearly 1700 years we have ample testimonies to the effectiveness of this animistic archetype. Mercurius is on the one hand a metal, on the other a fluid that can easily be volatilized, i.e., changed into vapour or spirit; this was known as *spiritus Mercurii* and was regarded as a kind of panacea, saviour, and *servator mundi* (preserver of the world). Mercurius is a "bringer of healing" who "makes peace between enemies"; as the "food of immortality" he saves Creation from sickness and corruption, just as Christ saved mankind. In the language of the Church Fathers, Christ is a "springing fountain", and in the same way the alchemists call Mercurius *aqua permanens, ros Gedeonis* (Gideon's dew), *vinum ardens* (fiery wine), *mare nostrum* (our sea), *sanguis* (blood), etc.

From many of the reports, particularly the early ones, it is evident that the UFOs can appear suddenly and vanish equally suddenly. They can be tracked by radar but remain invisible to the eye, and conversely, can be seen by the eye but not detected by radar. UFOs can make themselves invisible at will, it is said, and must obviously consist of a substance that is visible at one moment and invisible the next. The nearest analogy to this is a volatile liquid which condenses out of an invisible state into the form of drops. In reading the old texts one can still feel the miracle of disappearance and reappearance which the alchemists beheld in the vaporization of water or quicksilver: for them it was the transformation of the "souls that had become water" (Heraclitus) into the invisible pneuma at the touch of Hermes' wand, and their descent out of the empyrean into visible form again. Zosimos of Panopolis (third century A.D.) has left us a valuable document describing this transformation, which takes place in a cooking-vessel. The fantasies born of musing over the steaming cooking-pot—one of the most ancient experiences of mankind—may also be responsible for the sudden disappearance and reappearance of the UFO.

The unexpected drop-form in our dream has prompted a comparison with a central conception of alchemy, known to us not only from Europe but also from India and second-century China. The extraordinariness of the UFOs is paralleled by the extraordinariness of its psychological context, which has to be adduced if we are to risk any interpretation at all. Considering the essential weirdness of the UFO phenomenon, we cannot expect the familiar, rationalistic principles of explanation to be in any way adequate. A psychoanalytic approach to the problem could do nothing more than turn the whole idea of UFOs into a sexual fantasy, at most arriving at the conclusion that a repressed uterus was coming down from the sky. This would not fit in too badly with the old medical view of hysteria (Gk. *hysteros*=womb) as a "wandering of the uterus", especially in the case of a woman who had an anxiety dream. But then, what about the masculine pilots, who are the chief authors of the rumour? The language of sex is hardly more significant than any other symbolical means of expression. This type of explanation is, at bottom, just as mythological and rationalistic as the technological fables about the nature and purpose of UFOs.

The dreamer knew enough about psychology to realize in her second dream the necessity of not giving in to her fear and running away, as she would dearly have liked to do. But the unconscious created a situation in which this way out was barred. Consequently she had an opportunity to observe the phenomenon at close quarters. It proved to be harmless. Indeed, the untroubled footsteps of a woman point to someone who either is not aware of it at all or is free from fear.

COMMENTARY TO DREAM 2

The exposition begins with the statement that it is night and dark, a time when normally everyone is asleep and dreaming. As in the previous dream, panic breaks out. A number of UFOs appear. Recalling the first commentary, we could say that the unity of the self as a supraordinate, semi-divine figure has broken up into a plurality. On a mythological level this would correspond to a plurality of gods, god-men, demons, or souls. In Hermetic philosophy the arcane substance has a "thousand names", but essentially it consists of the One and Only (i.e., God), and this principle only becomes pluralized through being split up (*multiplicatio*). The alchemists were consciously performing an *opus divinum* in that they sought to free the "soul in chains", i.e., to release the demiurge distributed and imprisoned in his own creation and restore him to his original condition of unity.

Looked at psychologically, the plurality of the symbol of unity signifies a splitting into many independent units, into a number of "selves"; the *one* "metaphysical" principle, representing the idea of monotheism, is dissolved into a plurality of subordinate deities. From the standpoint of Christian dogma such an operation could easily be construed as arch-heresy, were it not that this view is contradicted by the unequivocal saying of Christ: "Ye are gods", and by the equally emphatic idea that we are all God's children, both of which presuppose man's at least potential kinship with God. From the psychological point of view, however, the plurality of UFOs would correspond to the projection of a plurality of human individuals, the choice of symbol (spherical object) indicating that the content of the projection is not the actual people themselves, but rather their ideal psychic totality; not the empirical man as he knows himself to be from experience, but his whole psyche, the conscious contents of which have still to be supplemented by the contents of the unconscious. Although we know, from our investigations, a number of things about the unconscious which give us some clue as to its nature, we are still very far from being able to sketch out even a hypothetical picture that is in any way adequate. To mention only one of the greatest difficulties: there are parapsychological experiences which can no longer be denied and have to be taken into account in evaluating psychic processes. The unconscious can no longer be treated as if it were causally dependent on consciousness, since it possesses qualities which are not under conscious control. It should rather be understood as an autonomous entity acting reciprocally with consciousness.

The plurality of UFOs, then, is a projection of a number of psychic images of wholeness which appear in the sky because on the one hand they represent archetypes charged with energy and on the other hand are not recognized as psychic factors. The reason for this is that our present-day consciousness possesses no conceptual categories by means of which it could apprehend the nature of psychic totality. It is still in an archaic state, so to speak, in which apperceptions of this kind do not occur, and accordingly the relevant contents cannot be recognized as psychic factors. Moreover, it is so trained that it must think of such images not as forms inherent in the psyche but as existing somewhere in extra-psychic, metaphysical space, or else as historical facts. When, therefore, the archetype receives from the conditions of the time and from the general psychic situation an additional charge of energy, it cannot, for the reasons I have described, be integrated directly into consciousness, but is forced to manifest itself indirectly in the form of spontaneous projections. The projected image then appears as an ostensibly physical fact independent of the individual psyche and its nature. In other words, the rounded wholeness of the mandala becomes a space ship controlled by an intelligent being. The usually lens-shaped form of the UFOs may be helped by the fact that psychic wholeness, as the historical testimonies show, has always been characterized by certain cosmic affinities: the individual soul was thought to be of "heavenly" origin, a particle of the world soul, and hence a microcosm, a reflection of the macrocosm. Leibniz's Monadology is an eloquent example of this. The macrocosm is the starry world around us, which, appearing to the naïve mind as spherical, gives the soul its traditional spherical form. Actually the astronomical heavens are filled with mainly lens-shaped agglomerations of stars, the galaxies, similar in form to that of the UFOs. This form may possibly be a concession to the recent astronomical findings, for to my knowledge there are no older traditions that speak of the soul having the form of a lens. Here we may have an instance of an older tradition being modified by recent additions to knowledge, an influencing of primordial ideas by the latest acquisitions of consciousness, like the frequent substitution of automobiles and aeroplanes for animals and monsters in modern dreams.

It must be emphasized, however, that there is also the possibility of a natural or absolute "knowledge", where the unconscious psyche coincides with objective facts. This is a problem that has been raised by the discoveries of parapsychology. "Absolute knowledge" occurs not only in telepathy and pre-cognition, but also in biology, for instance in the attunement of the virus of hydrophobia to the anatomy of dog and man as described by Portmann,[2] the wasp's apparent knowledge of where the motor ganglia are located in the caterpillar that is to nourish the wasp's progeny, the emission of light by certain fishes and insects, with almost 100 per cent efficiency, the directional sense of carrier pigeons, the warning of earthquakes given by chickens and cats, and the amazing co-operation found in symbiotic relationships. We know, too, that the life process itself cannot be explained only by causality, but requires "intelligent" choice. The shape of the UFOs is in this sense analogous to that of the elements

[2] A. Portmann, "The Significance of Images in the Living Transformation of Energy", *Eranos-Jahrbuch* 1952.

composing the structure of space, the galaxies, no matter how ridiculous this seems to human reason.

In our dream the usual lens-shaped form is replaced by the rarer cigar-form, derived apparently from the old dirigible airships. As in Dream 1 a psychoanalytic approach could resort to a female "symbol", the uterus, to explain the "drop", so here the sexual analogy of the phallic form leaps to the eye. The archaic background of the psyche has this much in common with primitive language, that they both translate unknown or incompletely understood things into instinctive and habitual forms of thought, so that Freud could, with some justification, establish that all round or hollow forms have a feminine and all oblong ones a masculine meaning, as for instance nuts and bolts, male and female pipe-joints, etc. In these cases the interest that naturally attaches to sex stimulates the making of such analogies, not to speak of the amusing illustrations they provide. Still, sex is not the sole instigator of these metaphors, there is also hunger, the urge to eat and drink. In the history of religion there are not only sexual unions with the gods, they are also eaten and drunk. Even sexual attraction has become the object of these metaphors: we like a girl so much that we could "eat" her. Language is full of metaphors which express one instinct in terms of another, but we need not conclude from this that the real and essential thing is always "love" or hunger or the urge to power, etc. The main point is that every situation activates the relevant instinct, which then dominates as a vital need and decides the choice of symbol as well as its interpretation.[3]

Very probably there is a phallic analogy in the dream, which, in accordance with the meaning of this exceedingly archaic symbol, gives the UFO the character of something "procreative",

[3] The phallus is not a sign that indicates the penis. It is a "symbol" because it has so many other meanings.

"fructifying" and, in the broadest sense, "penetrating".[4] In ancient times the feeling of being "penetrated" by, or of "receiving", the god was allegorized by the sexual act. But it would be a gross misunderstanding to interpret a genuine religious experience as a "repressed" sexual fantasy on account of a mere metaphor. The "penetration" can also be expressed by a sword, spear, or arrow.

The dreamer does not flee from the menacing aspect of the UFO, even when she sees it coming straight at her. During this confrontation the original spherical or lens-shaped aspect reappears in the form of a circular eye. This image corresponds to the traditional eye of God, which, all-seeing, searches the hearts of men, laying bare the truth and pitilessly exposing every cranny of the soul. It is a reflection of one's insight into the total reality of one's own being.

The eye is half blue, half white. This corresponds to the colours of the sky, its pure blue and the whiteness of clouds that obscure its transparency. The psychic totality, the self, is a combination of opposites. Without a shadow even the self is not real. It always has two aspects, a bright and a dark, like the pre-Christian idea of God in the Old Testament, which is so much better suited to the facts of religious experience (Rev. 14:7) than the Summum Bonum, based as this is on the precarious foundation of a mere syllogism (the *privatio boni*). Even the highly Christian Jacob Boehme could not escape this insight and gave eloquent expression to it in his "Forty Questions concerning the Soul".

The drop-shaped UFO, suggesting a fluid substance, a sort of "water", makes way for a circular structure which not only sees, i.e., emits light (according to the old view light is equivalent to seeing), but also sends out a scorching heat. One immediately thinks of the intolerable radiance that shone from the face of

---

[4] Dionysus, for instance, was invoked as *enkolpios*: "he in the lap".

Moses after he had seen God, of "who among us shall dwell with everlasting burnings" (Isaiah 33: 14), and of the saying of Jesus: "He who is near unto me is near unto the fire".

Nowadays people who have an experience of this kind are more likely to go running to the doctor or psychiatrist than to the theologian. I have more than once been consulted by people who were terrified by their dreams and visions. They took them for symptoms of mental illness, possibly heralding insanity, whereas in reality they were "dreams sent by God", real and genuine religious experiences that collided with a mind unprepared, ignorant, and profoundly prejudiced. In this matter there is little choice today: anything out of the ordinary can only be pathological, for that abstraction, the "statistical average", counts as the ultimate truth, and not reality. All feeling for value is repressed in the interests of a narrow intellect and biased reason. So it is no wonder that after her UFO experience our patient woke up in hospital with a burned face. This is only to be expected today.

The second dream differs from the first in that it brings out the dreamer's inner relationship to the UFO. The UFO has marked her out and not only turns a searching eye upon her but irradiates her with magical heat, a synonym for her own inner affectivity. Fire is the symbolical equivalent of a very strong emotion or affect, which in this case comes upon her quite unexpectedly. In spite of her justifiable fear of the UFO she held her ground, as though it were intrinsically harmless, but is now made to realize that it is capable of sending out a deadly heat, a statement we often meet with in the UFO literature.[5] This heat is a projection of her own unrealized emotion, that is, of a feeling that has intensified into an effect but remains unrecognized. Even her facial expression was altered (burnt) by it. This recalls not only the changed face of Moses but also that of Brother Klaus after his

---

[5] Cf. Keyhoe, The Flying Saucer Conspiracy, pp. 138f.

terrifying vision of God.[6] It points to an "indelible" experience whose traces remain visible to others, because it has brought about a demonstrable change in the entire personality. Psychologically, of course, such an event betokens only a *potential* change; it has first to be integrated into consciousness. That is why Brother Klaus felt it necessary to spend long years in wearisome study and meditation until he succeeded in recognizing his terrifying vision as a vision of the Holy Trinity, in accordance with the spirit of the age, thus transforming the experience into an integrated conscious content that was intellectually and morally binding for him. This work has still to be done by the dreamer, and perhaps also by all those who see UFOs, dream of them, or spread rumours about them.

The symbols of divinity coincide with those of the self: what, on the one side, appears as a psychological experience signifying psychic wholeness, expresses on the other side the idea of God. This is not to assert a metaphysical identity of the two, but merely the empirical identity of the images representing them, which all originate in the human psyche, as our dream shows. What the metaphysical conditions are for the similarity of the images is, like everything transcendental, beyond human knowledge.

The motif of the isolated "God's eye", which the unconscious proffers as an interpretation of the UFO, can be found in ancient Egyptian mythology as the "eye of Horus", who with its help healed the partial blinding of his father Osiris, caused by Set. The isolated God's eye also appears in Christian iconography.

In dealing with the products of the collective unconscious, all images that show an unmistakably mythological character have to be examined in their symbological context; they are the inborn language of the psyche and its structure, and, as regards their basic form, are in no sense individual acquisitions. Despite

[6] Cf. "Brother Klaus", *Psychology and Religion*, Coll. Works, vol. 11.

its capacity for learning and for consciousness, the human psyche is a natural phenomenon like the psyche of animals, and is based on inborn instincts which bring their own specific forms with them and in this way constitute the heredity of the species. Volition, intention, and all personal differentiations are acquired late and owe their existence to a consciousness that has emancipated itself from mere instinctivity. Wherever it is a question of archetypal formations, personalistic attempts at explanation lead us astray. The method of comparative symbology, on the other hand, not only proves fruitful on scientific grounds, but makes a deeper understanding possible in practice. The symbological or "amplificatory" approach produces a result that looks at first like a translation back into primitive language. And so it would be, if understanding with the help of the unconscious were a purely intellectual affair and not one that brought our total capacities into play. In other words, besides its formal mode of manifestation the archetype also possesses a numinous quality, a feeling-value that is highly effective in practice. One can be unconscious of this value, since it can be repressed artificially; but a repression has neurotic consequences, because the repressed affect still exists and simply makes an outlet for itself elsewhere, in some unsuitable place.

As our dream shows very clearly, the UFO comes from the unconscious background which has always expressed itself in numinous ideas and images. It is these that give the strange phenomenon an interpretation that makes it appear in a significant light—significant not merely because they arouse dim historical memories which link up with the findings of comparative psychology, but because actual affective processes are at work.

Today, as never before, men pay an extraordinary amount of attention to the skies, for technological reasons. This is especially true of the airman, whose field of vision is occupied on the one hand by the complicated control apparatus before him, and on the other by the empty vastness of cosmic space. His consciousness is concentrated one-sidedly on details requiring the most careful observation, while at his back, so to speak, his unconscious strives to fill the illimitable emptiness of space. His training and his common sense both preclude him from observing all the things that might rise up from within and become visible in order to compensate the emptiness and solitude of flight high above the earth. Such a situation provides the ideal conditions for spontaneous psychic phenomena, as everyone knows who has lived sufficiently long in the solitude, silence, and emptiness of deserts, seas, mountains, or in primeval forests. Rationalism and boredom are essentially products of the over-indulged craving for stimulation so characteristic of urban populations. The city-dweller seeks artificial sensations to escape his boredom; the hermit does not seek them, but is plagued by them against his will.

We know from the life of ascetics and anchorites that, whether they would or no, and without any assistance from consciousness, spontaneous psychic phenomena rose up to compensate their biological needs: numinous fantasy images, visions and hallucinations that were evaluated either positively or negatively. Those positively evaluated derived from a sphere of the unconscious felt to be spiritual, the others obviously from the instinctual world they knew only too well, where loaded dishes and flagons and luscious meals stilled their hunger, seductive and voluptuous beings yielded themselves to their pent-up sexual desires, riches and worldly power took the place of poverty and lack of influence, and bustling crowds, noise, and music enlivened the intolerable silence and loneliness. Although it is easy to speak here of images caused by repressed wishes and explain the projection of fantasies that way, it does not explain the visions that were evaluated positively, because these do not correspond to a repressed wish but to one that is fully conscious and therefore cannot produce a projection. A psychic content can only appear as a projection when its connection with the ego personality is not recognized. For this reason the wish hypothesis must be discarded.

The hermits sought to attain a spiritual experience and for this purpose they mortified the earthly man. Naturally enough the affronted world of instinct reacted with unseemly projections, but the spiritual sphere, too, responded with projections of a positive nature—most unexpectedly, to our scientific way of thinking. For the spiritual sphere had not been neglected in any way; on the contrary, it was nurtured with the greatest possible devotion through prayer, meditation, and other spiritual exercises. So, according to our hypothesis, it should have had no need of compensation; its one-sidedness, which insisted on mortifying the body, was already compensated by the violent reaction on the part of the instincts. Nevertheless the spontaneous appearance of positive projections in the form of numinous images was experienced as grace and felt to be a divine revelation, and indeed they are characterized as such by the content of the visions. Psychologically speaking, these visions behave in exactly the same way as the visions produced by the neglected instincts, despite the undeniable fact that the saints did everything to foster their spirituality. They did *not* mortify the spiritual man and therefore needed no compensation in this respect.

If, in the face of this dilemma, we cling to the proven truth of the compensation theory, we are driven to the paradoxical conclusion that, despite appearances to the contrary, the spiritual situation of the hermit was one of deficiency after all, and that it needed an appropriate compensation. Just as physical hunger is sated, at least metaphorically, by the sight of a marvellous meal, so the hunger of the soul is sated by the vision of numinous images. But it is not so easy to see why the anchorite's soul should suffer from "hunger". He stakes his whole life on earning the *panis supersubstantialis*, the "super-essential bread" which alone appeases his hunger, and besides that he has the faith, doctrines, and means of grace of the Church at his disposal. Why, then, should he lack anything? All this he has, but the fact remains that he is not nourished by it and his unappeasable desire remains unfulfilled. What, obviously, he still lacks is the *actual and immediate experience of spiritual reality*, however it may turn out. Whether it presents itself to him more or less concretely or symbolically makes little difference. In any case he is not expecting the physical tangibility of any earthly thing, but rather the sublime intangibleness of a spiritual vision. This experience is, in itself, a compensation for the barrenness and emptiness of traditional forms, and accordingly he values it above all else. For in fact there appears before him, uncreated by himself, a numinous image which is just as real and "actual" (because it "acts" upon him) as the illusions spun by his neglected instincts. It is, however, as much desired by him on account of its reality and spontaneity as the illusions of his senses are undesired. So long as the numinous contents can avail themselves, in one way or another, of the traditional forms, there is no cause for disquiet. But when they betray their archaism by assuming unusual and obnoxious features, the matter becomes painfully dubious. The saint then begins to doubt whether they are any less illusory than the delusions of the senses. Indeed, it may even happen that a revelation originally regarded as divine is subsequently damned as a deception of the devil. The criterion of distinction is simply and solely tradition, not reality or unreality as in the case of a real or illusory meal. The vision is a psychic phenomenon, just as are its numinous contents. Here spirit answers spirit, whereas in a fast the need for food is answered by an hallucination and not by a real meal. In the first case the bill is paid in cash, in the second case by an unbacked cheque. The one solution is satisfying, the other obviously not.

But in both cases the structure of the phenomenon is the same. Physical hunger needs a real meal and spiritual hunger

needs a numinous content. Such contents are by nature archetypal and have always expressed themselves in the form of natural revelations, for Christian symbolism, like all other religious
ideas, is based on archetypal models that go back into prehistory. The "total" character of these symbols includes every kind
of human interest and instinct, thereby guaranteeing the numinosity of the archetype. That is why, in comparative religion, we
so often find the religious and spiritual aspects associated with
those of sexuality, hunger, aggression, power, etc. A particularly
fruitful source of religious symbolism is the instinct to which
most importance is attached in a given epoch or culture, or
which is of most concern to the individual. There are com-
munities in which hunger is more important than sex and vice
versa. Our civilization bothers us less with food taboos than with
sexual restrictions. In modern society these have come to play
the role of an injured deity that is getting its own back in every
sphere of human activity, including psychology, where it would
reduce "spirit" to sexual repression.

However, a partial interpretation of the symbolism in sexual
terms should be taken seriously. If the striving for a spiritual
goal is not a genuine instinct but merely the result of a particular
social development, then an explanation according to sexual
principles is the most appropriate and the most acceptable to
reason. But even if we grant the striving for wholeness and unity
the character of a genuine instinct, and base our explanation
mainly on this principle, the fact still remains that there is a close
association between sexual instinct and the striving for wholeness. With the exception of religious longings, nothing challenges modern man more consciously and personally than sex.
One can also say in good faith that he is possessed even more by
the power instinct. This question will be decided according to
temperament and one's own subjective bias. The only thing we
cannot doubt is that the most important of the fundamental
instincts, the religious instinct for wholeness, plays the least

conspicuous part in contemporary consciousness because, as history shows, it can free itself only with the greatest effort, and with continual backslidings, from contamination with the other two instincts. These can constantly appeal to common, everyday facts known to everyone, but the religious instinct requires for its evidence a more highly differentiated consciousness, thoughtfulness, reflection, responsibility, and sundry other virtues. Therefore it does not commend itself to the relatively unconscious man driven by his natural impulses, because, imprisoned in his familiar world, he clings to the commonplace, the obvious, the probable, the collectively valid, using for his motto: "Thinking is difficult, therefore let the herd pronounce judgment!" It is an enormous relief to him when something that looks complicated, unusual, puzzling and problematical can be reduced to something ordinary and banal, especially when the solution strikes him as surprisingly simple and somewhat droll. The most convenient explanations are invariably sex and the power instinct, and reduction to these two dominants gives rationalists and materialists an ill-concealed satisfaction: they have neatly disposed of an intellectually and morally uncomfortable difficulty, and on top of that can enjoy the feeling of having accomplished a useful work of enlightenment which will free the individual from unnecessary moral and social burdens. In this way they can pose as benefactors of mankind. On closer inspection, however, things look very different: the exemption of the individual from a difficult and apparently insoluble task drives sexuality into an even more pernicious repression, where it is replaced by rationalism or by devastating cynicism, while the power instinct is driven towards some Socialistic ideal that has already turned half the world into the State prison of Communism. This is the exact opposite of what the striving for wholeness wants, namely to free the individual from the compulsion of the other two instincts. The task before him comes back with all its energies unused, and reinforces, to an almost pathological degree, the very instincts that have always stood in the way of man's higher development. At all events it has a neuroticizing effect characteristic of our time and must bear most of the blame for the splitting of the individual and of the world in general. We just will not admit the shadow, and so the right hand does not know what the left is doing.

Correctly appraising the situation, the Catholic Church, while counting sexual sins among the "venial" ones, therefore keeps a sharp eye upon sexuality as the chief enemy in practice and ferrets it out in all corners. She thus creates an acute consciousness of sex, deleterious to weaker spirits but of advantage in promoting reflection and broadening the consciousness of the stronger. The worldly pomps of the Catholic Church for which she is reproached by the Protestants have the obvious purpose of keeping the power of the spirit visibly before the natural power instinct. This is infinitely more effective than the best logical arguments, which no one likes following. Only the tiniest fraction of the population learn anything from reflection; everything else consists in the suggestive power of example.

After this digression, let us turn back to the problem of sexual interpretation.

If we try to define the psychological structure of the religious experience which saves, heals, and makes whole, the simplest formula we can find would seem to be the following: *in religious experience man comes face to face with a psychically overwhelming Other*. As to the existence of this power we have only assertions, but no physical or logical proofs. It comes upon man in psychic guise. We cannot explain it as exclusively spiritual, for experience would immediately compel us to retract such a judgment, since the vision, according to the psychic disposition of the individual, often assumes the form of sexuality or of some other unspiritual impulse. Only something overwhelming, no matter what form of expression it uses, can challenge the whole man and force him to react as a whole. It cannot be proved that such things happen or that they must occur, nor is there any proof that they are anything more than psychic,[7] since the evidence for them rests solely on personal statements and avowals. This, in view of the crass undervaluation of the psyche in our predominantly materialistic and statistical age, sounds like a condemnation of religious experience. Consequently, the average intelligence takes refuge either in unbelief or in credulity, for to it the psyche is no more than a miserable wisp of vapour. Either there are hard-and-fast facts, or else it is nothing but illusion begotten by repressed sexuality or an over-compensated inferiority complex. As against this I have urged that the psyche be recognized as having its own peculiar reality. Despite the advances in organic chemistry, we are still very far from being able to explain consciousness as a biochemical process. On the contrary, we have to admit that chemical laws do not even explain the selective process of food assimilation, let alone the self-regulation and self-preservation of the organism. Whatever the reality of the psyche may be, it seems to coincide with the reality of life and at the same time to have a connection with the formal laws governing the inorganic world. For the psyche has yet another property which most of us would rather not admit, namely, that peculiar factor which relativizes space and time, and is now the object of intensive parapsychological research.

Since the discovery of the empirical unconscious the psyche and what goes on in it have become a natural fact and are no longer an arbitrary opinion, which they undoubtedly would be if they owed their existence to the caprices of a rootless consciousness. But consciousness, for all its kaleidoscopic mobility, rests as we know on the comparatively static or at least highly conservative foundation of the instincts and their specific forms,

[7] Neither is there any proof that they are "only" psychic!

the archetypes. This world in the background[8] proves to be the opponent of consciousness, which, because of its mobility (learning capacity), is often in danger of losing its roots. That is why since the earliest times men have felt compelled to perform rites for the purpose of securing the co-operation of the unconscious. In a primitive world no one reckons without his host; he is constantly mindful of the gods, the spirits, of fate and the magical qualities of time and place, rightly recognizing that man's solitary will is only a fragment of a total situation. Primitive man's actions have a "total" character which civilized man would like to be rid of, as though it were an unnecessary burden. Things seem to go all right without it.

The great advantage of this attitude lies in the development of a discriminating consciousness, but it has the almost equally great disadvantage of breaking down man's original wholeness into separate functions which conflict with one another. This loss has made itself increasingly felt in modern times. I need only remind you of Nietzsche's Dionysian experience of a "breakthrough", and of that trend in German philosophy whose most obvious symptom is the book by Ludwig Klages, *The Spirit as the Adversary of the Soul*. Through this fragmentation process one or other of the functions of consciousness becomes highly differentiated and can then escape the control of the other functions to such an extent that it attains a kind of autonomy, constructing a world of its own into which these other functions are admitted only so far as they can be subjugated to the dominant function. In this way consciousness loses its balance: if the intellect predominates, then the value judgments of feeling are weakened,

---

[8] Here I must beg the reader to eschew the popular misconception that this background is "metaphysical". This view is a piece of gross carelessness of which even professional people are guilty. It is far more a question of instincts which influence not only our outward behaviour but also the psychic structure. The psyche is not an arbitrary fantasy; it is a biological fact subject to the laws of life.

and vice versa. Again, if sensation is predominant, intuition is barred, this being the function that pays the least attention to tangible facts; and conversely, a man with an excess of intuition lives in a world of unproven possibilities. A useful result of such developments is specialism, but that also promotes a disagreeable one-sidedness.

It is just this capacity for one-sidedness which bids us observe things from one angle only, and if possible to reduce them to a single principle. In psychology this attitude inevitably leads to explanations in terms of one particular bias. For instance, in a case of marked extraversion the whole of the psyche is traced back to environmental influences, while in introversion it is traced back to the hereditary psychophysical disposition and the intellectual and emotional factors that go with it. Both explanations tend to turn the psychic apparatus into a machine. Anyone who tries to be equally fair to both points of view is accused of obscurantism. Yet both of them should be applied, even if a series of paradoxical statements is the result. Hence, in order to avoid multiplying the principles of explanation, one of the easily recognizable basic instincts will be preferred at the expense of the others. Nietzsche bases everything on power, Freud on pleasure and its frustration. While in Nietzsche the unconscious can be felt as a factor of some importance, and in Freud became a *sine qua non* of his theory, though without ever sloughing off the character of being something secondary and "nothing but" the result of repression, in Adler the field of vision is narrowed down to a subjective "prestige"-psychology, where the unconscious as a possibly decisive factor disappears from sight altogether. This fate has also overtaken Freud's psychoanalysis as practised by the second generation. The significant beginnings he made towards a psychology of the unconscious stopped short at a single archetype, that of the Oedipus complex, and were not developed further by the more rigorous of his pupils.

The evidence for the sexual instinct is, in the case of an incest complex, so patently obvious that a philosophically limited intelligence could be satisfied with that. The same is true of Adler's subjective will to power. Both views remain caught in an instinctual premise which leaves no room for the other and so lands us in the specialist *cul de sac* of fragmentary explanation. Freud's pioneer work, on the other hand, gave access to the well-documented history of psychic phenomenology, and this allows us something like a synoptic view of the psyche. The psyche does not express itself merely in the narrow subjective sphere of the individual personality but, over and above that, in collective psychic phenomena of whose existence Freud was aware, at least in principle, as his concept of the "superego" shows. For the time being, however, method and theory will remain in the hands of the psychiatrist, who of necessity is concerned only with individuals and their urgent personal problems. An investigation of fundamentals involving historical research is naturally not in his line, nor are his scientific training and his practical work of much help to him in getting at the foundations of psychological knowledge. For this reason even Freud saw himself obliged to skip the—admittedly—wearisome stage of comparative psychology and press forward into the conjectural and highly uncertain prehistory of the human psyche. In so doing he lost the ground from under his feet, for he would not let himself be taught by the findings of ethnologists and historians, but transferred the insights he had gained from modern neurotics during consulting hours directly to the broad field of primitive psychology. He did not pay enough attention to the fact that under certain conditions there is a shift of emphasis and other psychic dominants come into play. The Freudian school got stuck at the Oedipus motif, i.e., the archetype of incest, and hence their views remained predominantly sexualistic. They failed to recognize that the Oedipus complex is an exclusively masculine affair, that sexuality is not the only possible dominant in the psychic process, and that incest, because it involves the religious instinct, is far more an expression of the latter than the cause of it. I will not mention my own endeavours in this field, since for most people they have remained a book with seven seals.

The sexual hypothesis nevertheless possesses considerable power of conviction because it coincides with one of the principal instincts. The same is true of the power hypothesis, which can appeal to instincts that characterize not only the individual but also political and social movements. A *rapprochement* between the two standpoints is nowhere in sight, unless we can acknowledge the peculiar nature of the self, which embraces the individual as well as society. As experience shows, the archetypes possess the quality of "transgressiveness"; they can sometimes manifest themselves in such a way that they seem to belong as much to society as to the individual; they are therefore numinous and contagious in their effects. (It is the emotional person who emotionalizes others.) In certain cases this transgressiveness also produces meaningful coincidences, i.e., acausal, synchronistic phenomena, such as the results of Rhine's ESP experiments.

The instincts are part of the living totality; they are articulated with and subordinate to the whole. Their release as separate entities leads to chaos and nihilism, because it breaks down the unity and totality of the individual and destroys him. It should be the task of psychotherapy, properly understood, to preserve or restore this unity. It cannot be the aim of education to turn out rationalists, materialists, specialists, technicians and others of the kind who, unconscious of their origins, are precipitated abruptly into the present and contribute to the disorientation and fragmentation of society. By the same token, no psychotherapy can lead to satisfactory results if it confines itself to single aspects only. The temptation to do this is so great, and the danger of loss of instinct so threatening in the breathless tempo of modern civilization, that every expression of instinct must be watched very carefully, since it is part of the total picture and is essential for man's psychic balance.

For these reasons the sexual aspect of the UFOs merits our attention, as it shows that a very powerful instinct like sexuality has its share in the structure of the phenomenon. It is probably no accident that in one of the dreams a feminine symbol appears, and in the other a masculine, in accordance with the reports of lens-shaped and cigar-shaped UFOs, for where one appears, we may also expect its partner.

The vision is a symbol consisting not only of archetypal forms of thought but of instinctual elements, too, so that it can justly lay claim to be a "reality". It is not only "historical", but topical and dynamic. Hence it does not appeal only to man's conscious technological fantasies, or his philosophical speculations, but strikes deep down into his "animal" nature. This is what we would expect a genuine symbol to do; it must affect and express the whole man. However unsatisfactory a sexual interpretation may be in this case, the contribution it makes should not be overlooked and must be given due consideration.

In the same way the power instinct expresses itself in both dreams; the dreamer appears in a unique situation, she is singled out, indeed "chosen" like one whose countenance is burned by the divine fire. Both interpretations, so far as they claim to be exclusive, do away with the symbolic meaning of the dreams and eliminate the individual in favour of the instinctual manifestations. The feebleness of the individual in the face of the overwhelming power of instinct is once more established. For anyone who was not yet aware of this fact, such an interpretation would of course be novel and impressive. But our dreamer does not belong to the host of ingénues, and in her case it would be pointless to reduce the dream in this way. She is, on the contrary, one of those moderns who realize what the elimination of the individual means. The paralyzing feeling of nothingness and lostness is compensated by the dreams: she is the only one to withstand the panic and to recognize its cause. It is at her that the unearthly thing points, and on her it leaves the visible traces of its power. She is set apart as one of the elect. Such a gesture on the part of the unconscious naturally has a useful meaning only when feelings of inferiority and the senselessness of a merely functional existence threaten to stifle the personality.

This case may serve as a paradigm for the widespread anxiety and insecurity of thoughtful people today, while at the same time revealing the compensating power of the unconscious.

DREAM 3

This dream is an excerpt from a longer dream which a 42-year-old woman patient recorded about six years ago. At the time she had heard nothing of Flying Saucers and the like.

She dreamt she was standing in a garden, when suddenly the humming of an engine became audible overhead. She sat down on the garden wall in order to see what was going on. A black metallic object appeared and circled over her: it was a huge flying spider made of metal, with great dark eyes. It was round in shape, and was a new and unique aeroplane. From the body of the spider there issued a solemn voice, loud and distinct; it uttered a prayer that was intended as an admonition and a warning to everybody, for those on earth as well as for the occupants of the spider. The gist of the prayer was: "Lead us downwards and keep us (safe) below ... Carry us up to the height!" Adjoining the garden was a large administrative building where international decisions were being taken. Flying incredibly low, the spider passed along the windows of the building, for the obvious purpose of letting the voice influence the people inside and point out the way to peace, which was the way to the inner, secret world. They were to take reconciling decisions. There were several other spectators in the garden.

> She felt somewhat embarrassed because she was not fully clothed.

COMMENTARY TO DREAM 3 .

In the preceding part of the dream the dreamer's bed had stood close to the garden wall. In her dream, therefore, she had slept under the open sky and been exposed to the free influences of Nature, which means psychologically the impersonal, collective unconscious, for this forms the counterpart to our natural environment and is always projected upon it. The wall denotes a barrier separating the immediate world of the dreamer from a more distant one (administrative building). A round metallic object appears, described as a flying spider. This description fits the UFOs. As regards the designation "spider", we are reminded of the hypothesis that UFOs are a species of insect coming from another planet and possessing a shell or case that shines like metal. An analogy would be the metallic-looking, chitinous covering of our beetles. Each UFO is supposed to be a single insect, not a swarm.[9] In reading the numerous reports I must admit that I, too, was struck by the thought that the peculiar behaviour of the UFOs was reminiscent of certain insects. To the speculative mind there is nothing inherently impossible in the idea that under other conditions Nature could implement her "knowledge" in quite other ways than those mentioned earlier; for instance, instead of light-producing insects she might evolve creatures capable of "anti-gravity". In any case our technological imagination often lags a long way behind Nature's. Everything in our experience is subject to the law of gravity with one

[9] Sievers, *Flying Saucers über Südafrika*, p. 157, mentions Gerald Heard's hypothesis that they are a species of bees from Mars (*The Riddle of the Flying Saucers*, London, 1950). Harold T. Wilkins, in *Flying Saucers on the Moon*, mentions a report on a "rain of threads", supposed to come from unknown spiders.

great exception: the psyche, which, as we experience it, is weightlessness itself. The psychic "object" and gravity are, to the best of our knowledge, incommensurable. They seem to be different in principle. The psyche represents the only opposite of gravity known to us. It is "anti-gravity" in the truest sense of the world. In corroboration of this we could cite the parapsychological experience of levitation and other psychic phenomena, denied only by the ignorant, which relativize time and space.

Obviously the "flying spider" is based on an unconscious fantasy of this kind. In the UFO literature, too, reference is made to flying spiders in an attempt to explain the alleged "rain of threads" in Oloron and Gaillac.[10] Note that the dream cannot help making a concession to modern technological fantasies: it calls the spider a "new and unique aeroplane".

The psychic nature of the spider is shown by the fact that it contains a "voice", evidently issuing from something like a human being. This curious phenomenon reminds one of similar occurrences in insane people, who can hear voices issuing from anything or anybody. "Voices", like visions, are autonomous manifestations of the senses caused by the activity of the unconscious. "Voices from the aether" also occur in the UFO literature.[11]

Emphasis is laid on the eyes, which denote seeing and the intention to see. The intention is expressed by the voice, whose message is addressed both to the earth dwellers and to the "occupants of the spider". The association with "aeroplane" here gives rise to the illogical idea of a machine that transports passengers. The passengers are evidently thought of as quasi-human, for the message is meant for them as well as for human beings. We can therefore suppose that both are simply different

[10] Aimé Michel, *The Truth about Saucers.*
[11] Wilkins, p. 138.

aspects of man, e.g., the empirical man below on earth and the spiritual man in heaven.

The cryptic message or "prayer" is spoken by a single voice, by a kind of prayer leader. He addresses himself to that which "leads" and "carries", and this must be the spider. We are therefore obliged to examine the symbol of the spider somewhat more closely. As we know, although this animal is quite harmless in our latitudes, it is for many people an object of horror and superstitious belief (*araignée du matin, grand chagrin; araignée du soir, grand espoir*).[12] When someone is not quite right in the head, we say in German that he "spins" and "has cobwebs in the attic". Spiders, like all animals that are not warm-blooded or have no cerebrospinal nervous system, function in dreams as symbols of a profoundly alien psychic world. So far as I can see, they express contents which, though active, are unable to reach consciousness; they have not yet entered the sphere of the cerebrospinal nervous system, but are as though lodged in the deeper-lying sympathetic and parasympathetic systems. In this connection I remember the dream of a patient who had the greatest difficulty in conceiving the idea of a supraordinate totality of the psyche and felt the utmost resistance to it. He had picked up the idea from one of my books but, characteristically enough, was unable to distinguish between the ego and the self, and, because of his hereditary taint, was threatened with a pathological inflation. In this situation he dreamt that he was rummaging about in the attic of his house, looking for something. In one of the attic windows he discovered a beautiful cobweb, with a large garden-spider sitting in the centre. It was of a blue colour, and its body sparkled like a diamond.

The dreamer was deeply impressed by this dream, and it was, in fact, an impressive commentary on his identification with the

---

[12] The horror people feel for spiders has been vividly described by Jeremias Gotthelf in his story, *The Black Spider* (London, 1958).

self—all the more dangerous in view of his heredity. In such cases there is a real weakness of the ego, which cannot therefore afford any suggestion of taking second place, as that would fatally emphasize its littleness and has to be avoided at all costs. Illusions, however, are inimical to life, because they are unhealthy, and sooner or later you will trip over them. The dream therefore attempts a kind of corrective, which, like the Delphic oracle, turns out to be ambivalent. It says in effect: "What is troubling you in the head (attic) is, though you may not know it, a rare jewel. It is like an animal that is strange to you, forming symbolically the centre of many concentric circles, reminiscent of the centre of a large or small world, like the eye of God in medieval pictures of the universe." Confronted with this, a healthy mind would fight against identification with the centre, because of the danger of paranoiac God-likeness. Anyone who gets into this spider's net is wrapped round like a cocoon and robbed of his own life. He is isolated from his fellows, so that they can no longer reach him, nor he them. He lives in the loneliness of the world creator, who is everything and has nothing outside himself. If, on top of all this, you have had an insane father, there is the danger that you will begin to "spin" yourself, and for this reason the spider has a sinister aspect that should not be overlooked.

The round metallic spider of our dreamer probably has a similar meaning. It has obviously devoured a number of human beings already, or their souls, and might well be a danger to earth dwellers. That is why the prayer, which recognizes the spider as a "divine" being, requests it to lead the souls "downwards" and "keep them safe below", because they are not yet departed spirits but living earthly creatures. As such they are meant to fulfil their earthly existence with conviction and not allow themselves any spiritual inflation, otherwise they will end up in the belly of the spider. In other words, they should not set the ego in the highest place and make it the ultimate authority, but should ever be mindful of the fact that it is not sole master in its own house and is surrounded on all sides by the factor we call the unconscious. What this is in itself we do not know. We know only its paradoxical manifestations. It is our business to under-stand Nature, and it is no good getting impatient with it because it is so "complicated" and awkward. Not so very long ago there were medical authorities who did not "believe" in bacteria and consequently allowed twenty thousand young women die of easily avoidable puerperal fever in Germany alone. The psychic catastrophes caused by the mental inertia of "experts" do not appear in any statistics, and from this it is concluded that they are non-existent.

The exhortation to remain below on earth is immediately followed by the paradoxical request: "Carry us up to the height!" One might think of the saying in *Faust*: "Then to the depths! I could as well say height: It's all the same", were it not that the dreamer has clearly separated the two processes by an hiatus. This shows that it is a sequence and not a *coincidentia oppositorum*. Evidently a moral process is envisaged, a katabasis and anabasis: the seven steps downwards and the seven steps upwards, the immersion in the *krater* followed by the ascent to the "heavenly generation" in the transformation mysteries. The Mass, too, begins with the "Confiteor quia peccavi nimis" . . . Apparently one has to be "led" downwards, because it is not easy for people to descend from their heights and remain below. In the first place a loss of social prestige is feared, and in the second a loss of moral self-esteem when they have to admit their own darkness. Hence they avoid self-criticism to an amazing degree, preach to others, and know nothing of themselves. They are happy to pos-sess no self-knowledge, because then nothing disturbs the rosy glow of illusions. "Below" means the bed-rock of reality, which despite all self-deceptions is there right enough. To get down to this and remain there seems to be a matter of pressing import-ance if it is assumed that people today are living above their proper level. An inference of such general scope is permitted by the dream, which shows the problem in terms of a human group and therefore characterizes it as a collective problem. Actually the dream has the whole of humanity in view, for the spider flies as near as possible to the windows of a building where "international decisions" are being taken. It tries to "influence" the meeting and point the way that leads to the "inner world", the way to self-knowledge. The dream expects that this will make peace possible. Accordingly the spider plays the role of a saviour who warns and brings a healing message.

At the end the dreamer discovers that she is insufficiently clothed. This very common dream motif usually indicates lack of adaptation or relative unconsciousness of the situation in which one finds oneself. This reminder of one's own fallibility and negligence is particularly appropriate at a time when other people are being enlightened, for in such cases there is always a lurking danger of inflation.

The admonition to "remain below" has in our day given rise to theological apprehensions in various quarters. It is feared that this kind of psychology will result in a loosening of moral standards. Psychology, however, gives us a clearer knowledge not only of evil but also of good, and the danger of succumbing to the former is considerably less than when you remain unconscious of it. Nor is psychology always needed if you want to know evil. No one who goes through the world with open eyes can ignore it; moreover he is not so likely to fall into a pit as the blind man. Just as the investigation of the unconscious is suspected by theologians of Gnosticism, so an inquiry into the ethical problems it raises is accused of antinomianism and libertinism. No one in his right senses would suppose that, after a thorough confession of sin accompanied by repentance, he will never sin again. It is a thousand to one that he will sin again the very next minute. Deeper psychological insight shows, in fact, that one cannot live at all without sinning "in thought, word, and deed". Only an exceedingly naïve and unconscious person could imagine that he is in a position to avoid sin. Psychology can no longer afford childish illusions of this kind; it must ensure the truth and declare that unconsciousness is not only no excuse but is actually one of the most heinous sins. Human law may exempt it from punishment, but Nature avenges herself the more mercilessly, for it is nothing to her whether a man is conscious of his guilt or not. We even learn from the parable of the unjust steward that the Lord praised his servant who kept a false account because he had "done wisely", not to speak of the (expurgated) passage at Luke 6, where Christ says to the defiler of the Sabbath: "Man, if indeed thou knowest what thou doest, thou art blessed; but if thou knowest not, thou art accursed, and a transgressor of the law".

Increased knowledge of the unconscious brings a deeper experience of life and greater consciousness, and therefore confronts us with apparently new situations that require ethical decision. These situations had, of course, always existed, but were not clearly grasped, either intellectually or morally, and were often left in a not unintentional half light. In this way one provides oneself with an alibi and can get out of an ethical decision. But, with deeper self-knowledge, one is often confronted with the most difficult problems of all, namely conflicts of duty, which simply cannot be decided by any moral precepts, neither those of the decalogue nor of other authorities. This is where ethical decisions really begin, for the mere observance of a codified "Thou shalt not" is not in any sense an ethical decision, but merely an act of obedience and, in certain circumstances, a convenient loophole that has nothing to do with ethics. In my long experience I have never encountered a situation that made a denial of ethical principles easier for me or raised the slightest doubt in this regard; on the contrary, the ethical problem was sharpened with increasing experience and insight, and the moral responsibility became more acute. It has become clear to me that, in contrast to the general view, unconsciousness is no excuse but is far rather a transgression in the literal sense of the word. Although there are, as mentioned above, allusions to this problem in the gospels, the Church has for understandable reasons not taken it up, but left the Gnostics to tackle it more seriously. As a result, Christians rely on the doctrine of the *privatio boni* and always think they know what is good and what is evil, thus substituting the moral code for the truly ethical decision, which is a *free* one. Morality consequently degenerates into legalistic behaviour, and the *felix culpa* remains stuck in the Garden of Eden. We are surprised at the decay of ethics in our century, and we contrast the standstill in this field with the progress of science and technology. But nobody is worried by the fact that a real ethos has disappeared behind a mass of moral precepts. An ethos, however, is a difficult thing that cannot be formulated and codified; it is one of those creative irrationalities upon which any true progress is based. It demands the whole man and not just a differentiated function.

The differentiated function undoubtedly depends on man, on his diligence, patience, perseverance, his striving for power, and his native gifts. With the aid of these things he gets on in the world and "develops". From this he has learnt that development and progress depend on man's own endeavours, his will and ability. But that is only one side of the picture. The other side shows man as he is and as he finds himself to be. Here he can alter nothing, because he is dependent on factors outside his control. Here he is not the doer, but a product that does not know how to change itself. He does not know how he came to be the unique individual he is, and he has only the scantiest knowledge of himself. Until recently he even thought that his psyche consisted of what he knew of himself and was a product of the cerebral cortex. The discovery of unconscious psychic processes more than fifty years ago is still far from being common knowledge and its implications are still not recognized. Modern man still does not realize that he is entirely dependent on the co-operation of the unconscious, which can actually cut short the very next sentence he proposes to speak. He is unaware that he is continuously sustained by something, while all the time he regards himself exclusively as the doer. He depends on and is sustained by an entity he does not know, but of which he has intimations that "occurred" or—as we can fitly say— revealed themselves to long forgotten forebears in the grey dawn of history. Whence did they come? Obviously from the unconscious processes, from that so-called unconscious which still precedes consciousness in every new human life, as the mother precedes the child. The unconscious depicts itself in dreams and visions, as it always did, holding before us images which, unlike the fragmented functions of consciousness, emphasize facts that relate to the unknown whole man, and only apparently to the function which interests us to the exclusion of all else. Although dreams usually speak the language of our par- ticular specialism—*canis panem somniat, piscator pisces*[13]—they refer to the whole, or at the very least to what man also is, namely the utterly dependent creature he finds himself to be.

In his striving for freedom man feels an almost instinctive aversion to this kind of knowledge, for he fears, not without reason, its paralysing effect. He may admit that this dependence on unknown powers exists—no matter what they are called— but he turns away from them as speedily as possible, as from a threatening obstacle. So long as everything appears to go well, this attitude may even be an advantage; but things do not always turn out for the best, particularly today, when despite euphoria and optimism we feel a tremor running through the foundations of our world. Our dreamer is certainly not the only person to feel afraid. Accordingly the dream depicts a collective need and utters a collective warning that we should descend to earth and not rise up again unless the spider carries up those who remain

[13] "The dog dreams of food, the fisherman of fish."

below. For when functionalism dominates consciousness, it is the unconscious that contains the compensatory symbol of wholeness. This, as I said, is represented by the image of the flying spider, which carries the one-sidedness and fragmentariness of the conscious mind. There is no development upwards unless it is facilitated by the unconscious. The conscious will alone cannot compel this creative act, and in order to illustrate this the dream chooses the symbol of prayer. Since according to the Pauline view we do not rightly know what we should pray for, the prayer is no more than a "groaning in travail" (Rom. 8: 22) which expresses our impotence. This enjoins on us an attitude that compensates the superstitious belief in man's will and ability. At the same time the spider image denotes a regression of religious ideas to the theriomorphic symbol of supreme power, a reversion to the long-forgotten stage where a monkey or a hare personifies the redeemer. Today the Christian Lamb of God or the Dove of the Holy Ghost has, at most, the value of a metaphor. As against this it must be emphasized that in dream symbolism animals refer to instinctual processes which play a vital part in animal biology. It is these processes which determine and shape the life of an animal. For his everyday life man seems to need no instincts, especially when he is convinced of the sovereign power of his will. He ignores the meaning of instinct and devalues it to the point of atrophy, not seeing how much he endangers his very existence through loss of instinct. When therefore dreams emphasize instinct they are trying to fill a perilous gap in our adaptation to life.

Deviations from instinct show themselves in the form of affects, which in dreams are likewise expressed by animals. Hence uncontrolled affects are rightly regarded as bestial or primitive and should be avoided. But we cannot do this without repressing them, that is, without a splitting of consciousness. In reality we can never escape their power. Somewhere or other they will continue to operate even though they cannot be found in consciousness. At worst they manifest themselves in a neurosis or in an unconscious "arrangement" of inexplicable mishaps. The saint, who seems exempt from these weaknesses, pays for his immunity with the sufferings and abnegations of the earthly man, without which of course he would not be a saint. The lives of holy men show that the two sides cancel out. None can escape the chain of suffering that leads to sickness, old age and death. We can and should, for the sake of our humanity, "control" our affects and keep them in check, but we should know that we have to pay dearly for it. The choice of currency in which we wish to pay the tribute is—sometimes— even left to us.

Remaining down below and subordinating ourselves to a theriomorphic symbol, which seems very like an insult to our human dignity, means no more than that we should remain conscious of these simple truths and never forget that in point of anatomy and psychology the earthly man, for all his high flights, is first cousin to the anthropoids. Should it be granted to him, however, to develop into something higher without crippling his nature, he is reminded that this transformation is not his to command, for he is dependent on factors he cannot influence. He must content himself with a prayerful yearning and "groaning", in the hope that something may carry him upward, since he is not likely to make a success of the Münchhausen experiment. Through this attitude he constellates helpful and at the same time dangerous powers in the unconscious; helpful if he understands them, dangerous if he misunderstands them. Whatever names he may give to these creative powers and potentialities within him, their actuality remains unchanged. No one can stop a religious-minded person from calling them gods or daemons, or simply "God", for we know from experience that they act just like that. If certain people use the word "matter" in this connection, believing that they have said something, we must remind them that they have merely replaced an X by a Y and are no further forward than before. The only certain thing is our profound ignorance, which cannot even know whether we have come nearer to the solution of the great riddle or not. Nothing can carry us beyond an "It seems as if" except the perilous leap of faith, which we must leave to those who are gifted or graced for it. Every real or apparent step forward depends on an experience of facts, the verification of which is, as we know, one of the most difficult tasks the human mind has to face.

DREAM 4

While I was engaged on this paper an acquaintance from abroad unexpectedly sent me a dream he had had on May 27th 1957. Our relationship was limited to one letter each every one or two years. He was an amateur astrologer and was interested in the question of synchronicity. He knew nothing of my preoccupation with UFOs, nor did he connect his dream in any way with the theme that interested me. His sudden and unusual decision to send me the dream comes, rather, into the category of meaningful coincidences, which statistical prejudice dismisses as irrelevant.

This is the dream:

It was late afternoon or early evening, the sun low on the horizon. The sky was cloudy, and there was a veil of cloud over the sun which did not, however, prevent one from seeing quite clearly his disk in outline behind the cloud. Under such circumstances the sun was white. Suddenly he took on an aspect of extraordinary pallor. The whole western horizon became a dreadful pale white. And the pallor—pallor is the word that I want to stress—of the orb of day became a terrifying wanness. Then a second sun appeared in the west about the same distance above the horizon, only a little more to the north. But as we gazed intently at the sky—there were a great number of people spread over a wide area watching the heavens as I was—the second sun took on the distinctive form of a sphere in contrast with the sun's disk, or apparent disk. Simultaneously with the setting of the sun and the advent of night the sphere came speeding towards the earth.

With the coming of the night, the whole potential of the dream was changed. Whereas words like pallor and wanness exactly describe the vanishing life, strength or potential of the sun, the sky now assumed an aspect of strength and majesty, which inspired not fear but *awe*. I could not say that I saw any stars, but the night sky was of that kind when thin wreaths of cloud allow an occasional star to be seen. The night certainly spoke of majesty, power and beauty.

When the sphere approached the earth at high velocity, I thought at first that it was Jupiter in aberration from its proper orbit, but as the sphere came nearer, I saw that, though large, it was much too small for Jupiter.

And it now became possible to discern the markings on its surface which were lines of longitude or like such, but were decorative and *symbolic* in character rather than geographical or mathematical. The beauty of the sphere, a subdued grey or opaque white, against the night sky must be emphasized. When we became aware that the sphere must certainly make a terrific impact upon the earth, we did, of course, feel fear, but it was fear in which *awe* was more predominant. It was a most awe-inspiring cosmic phenomenon. As we gazed, another and yet another sphere emerged from the horizon and sped towards the earth. Each sphere did in turn crash much as a bomb would crash, but at such a considerable distance that I, at least, could not make out the nature of the explosion or detonation or whatever it was. I think in one case, at least, I saw a flash. These spheres, then, were falling at intervals all around, but all of them . . . well beyond the point at which they might annihilate us. There appeared to be a danger of shrapnel. . . .

Then I must have gone indoors, for I found myself talking to a girl seated in a wicker chair, with an open large-paged notebook on her lap, much engrossed in her work. We were going—the rest of us—I think in a southwesterly direction, perhaps seeking safety, and I said to the girl had she better not come with us. The danger appeared to be great and we could hardly leave her alone there. She was quite definite in her reply. No, she would remain where she was and go on with her work. It was equally dangerous everywhere and one place was just as safe as another. I saw at once that she had reason and common sense on her side.

The dream ends by my being confronted with another girl, or, quite possibly, the same very competent and self-possessed young lady that I had left sitting in a wicker chair absorbed in her work. This time she was rather bigger and more realistic, and I could see her face, or at least that she was addressing me fairly and squarely. And she said in extraordinarily distinct tones: "J—S—, you will live till eleven eight." Nothing could surpass the clarity with which these eight words were articulated. Her authoritative way of enunciating them seemed to imply that I was to be censured for not supposing that I should live till eleven eight.

DREAMER'S COMMENTARY

This elaborate description was followed by the dreamer's comments, which can give us a number of hints as regards interpretation. As we should expect, he sees a climax in the sudden change of mood at the beginning of the dream, when the deathly, frightening pallor and wanness of the sunset changes into the sombre majesty of the night, and fear to awe. This, he said, was connected with his present preoccupation with the political future of Europe. On the basis of his astrological speculations he feared the coming of a World War in 1960–66. He had even felt impelled to write a letter to an eminent statesman expressing his fears. Afterwards he made the (not uncommon) discovery that his previously apprehensive and agitated mood suddenly changed into one of remarkable calm and even indifference, as though the whole affair no longer concerned him.

All the same, he could not explain to himself why the initial terror should be superseded by such a solemn and, as it were, holy mood. He felt certain, however, that it was a collective and not a personal matter, and he asked himself: "Are we to suppose that by hanging on too earnestly to the daylight of civilization we lose all potential, and that as we advance into what looks a fearful night there is more prospect of strength?" It is not very easy to fit the qualifying epithet "majesty" into such an interpretation. He himself related it to the fact that "the things that come from outer space are utterly beyond our control". "We might put it in theistic language by saying that it is utterly impossible to know the counsels of God and that in eternity the night is as significant as the day. Therefore our only possible chance is to accept the rhythm of eternity as night and day, and so the inexorable majesty of the night would become a source of strength." Evidently the dream underlines this characteristic defeatism by the cosmic interlude of a stellar bombardment to which mankind is helplessly exposed.

The dream contains no trace of sexuality if, as the dreamer said, we disregard the meeting with the young lady. (As if every relationship to the opposite sex was always necessarily based on sexuality!) What disturbed him was the fact that the meeting took place at night. One can carry "sex-consciousness" too far, as this remark shows. The wicker chair is not exactly inviting in this respect, and for the dreamer it signified an excellent condition for concentrated mental work, as indicated also by the note-book.

As the dreamer is an ardent student of astrology the combination of the numbers eleven and eight set him a special problem.

He thought of XI. 8 as the month and day of his decease. Being an elderly man of more than three-score years and ten he was thoroughly justified in such reflections. His astrological calculations led him to relegate this fatal November to the year 1963, the middle of the conjectural World War. But he added cautiously that he was by no means sure.

The dream, he said, left behind a strange feeling of contentment, and of thankfulness that such an experience had been "vouchsafed" him. It was, indeed, a "big" dream, for the like of which many a man has been thankful, even if he did not understand it correctly.

COMMENTARY TO DREAM 4

The dream begins with a sunset, when the sun is hidden by clouds so that all one can see is a disk. This would emphasize the round form, a tendency confirmed by the appearance of a second disk, Jupiter, more round bodies in large numbers, "things from outer space". For these reasons the dream comes into the category of psychic UFO phenomena.

The uncanny pallor of the sun is indicative of the fear that spreads over the daylight world in anticipation of catastrophic events to come. These events, much in contrast to his "daylight" views, are of unearthly origin: Jupiter, the father of the gods, has left his orbit and is approaching the earth. We meet this motif in Schreber's *Memoirs*: the extraordinary happenings going on all round him compel God to "move nearer to the earth". Here the unconscious "interprets" the threat as a divine intervention, which manifests itself in the appearance of smaller replicas of the great Jupiter. The dreamer does not draw the obvious conclusion about UFOs and does not seem to have been influenced in his choice of symbols by any conscious concern with them.

Although to all appearances a cosmic catastrophe is about to happen, the fear changes into a positive mood of a solemn, holy, and reverent kind, as is fitting for an epiphany. For the dreamer, however, the coming of the god signalizes extreme danger: the heavenly bodies explode on the earth like huge bombs, thus bearing out his fear of a World War. Remarkably enough, they do not cause the expected earthquake, and the detonations seem to be of a strange and unusual nature. No destruction takes place in the vicinity of the dreamer; the hits are so far below the horizon that all he thinks he can see is a single flash. The collision with these planetoids is therefore infinitely less dangerous than it would be in reality. The main point here seems to be fear of the possibility of a third World War, and it is this that gives the scene its terrifying aspect. It is the dreamer's own interpretation, rather than the phenomenon itself, which causes him to be so agitated. Consequently the whole affair assumes a markedly psychological aspect.

This is immediately borne out by the meeting with the young lady, who keeps her composure, imperturbably goes on with her work, and prophesies the date of his death. She does this in so solemn and impressive a manner that he even feels it necessary to emphasize the number of the words she uses, namely eight. That this figure is more than mere chance is proved by the supposed date of death—the 8th of November. This double emphasis on the eight is not without importance, for eight is a double quaternity and, as an individuation symbol in the mandalas, plays almost as great a role as the quaternity itself.[14] For lack of association material we shall suggest only a tentative interpretation of the number eleven with the help of the traditional symbolism. Ten is the perfect unfolding of unity, and the numbers one to ten have the significance of a completed cycle. $10 + 1 = 11$ therefore denotes the beginning of a new cycle. Since dream interpretation follows the principle *post hoc ergo propter hoc*, eleven leads to eight, the ogdoad, a totality symbol, and

---

[14] Cf. the Cabiri scene in *Faust; Psychology and Alchemy*, pp. 148ff.

hence to a realization of wholeness, as already suggested by the appearance of the UFOs.

The young lady, who seems to be unknown to the dreamer, may be taken as a compensating anima figure. She represents a more complete aspect of the unconscious than the shadow, since she adds to the personality its feminine traits. As a rule she appears most clearly when the conscious mind is thoroughly acquainted with its shadow, and she exerts her greatest influence as a psychological factor when the feminine qualities of the personality are not yet integrated. If these opposites are not united, wholeness is not established, and the self as their symbol is still unconscious. But when the self is constellated it appears in projection, though its true nature is hidden by the anima, who at most alludes to it, as in this dream: the anima, with her calmness and certainty, counters the agitations of the dreamer's ego consciousness, and by mentioning the number eight points to the totality, the self, which is present in the UFO projection.

The intuition of the enormous importance of the self as the organizer of the personality, and also of the collective dominants or archetypes, which as so-called metaphysical principles determine the orientation of consciousness, is responsible for the solemn mood prevailing at the beginning of the dream. It is a mood in keeping with the coming epiphany, though it is feared that this will unleash a World War or a cosmic catastrophe. The anima, however, seems to know better. Anyway the expected destruction remains invisible, there being no real cause for alarm in the dreamer's vicinity except his own subjective panic. The anima ignores his fear of a catastrophe and alludes instead to his own death, which we can well say is the real source of his fear.

Very often the nearness of death forcibly brings about a perfection that no effort of will and no good intentions could achieve. He is the great perfector, drawing his inexorable final line under the balance of human life. In him alone is wholeness—one way or another—attained. Death is the end of the empirical man and the goal of the spiritual man, as the perspicacious Heraclitus says: "It is to Hades that they rage and celebrate their feasts". Everything that is not yet where it ought to be, that has not yet gone where it ought to have gone, fears the end, the final reckoning. We avoid as long as possible making ourselves conscious of those things which wholeness still lacks, thus preventing ourselves from becoming conscious of the self and preparing for death. The self then remains in projection. In our dream it appears as Jupiter, which in approaching the earth changes into a multitude of smaller heavenly bodies, into numberless "selves" or individual souls, and vanishes in the earth, i.e., is integrated with our world. This hints, mythologically, at an incarnation, but psychologically it is the manifestation of an unconscious process in the sphere of consciousness.

Speaking in the language of the dream, I would advise the dreamer to consider the universal fear of catastrophe in the light of his own death. In this connection it is significant that the conjectured year of his death falls in the middle of the critical period 1960–66. The end of the world would therefore be his own death and hence, primarily, a personal catastrophe and a subjective end. But as the symbolism of the dream unmistakably portrays a collective situation, I think it would be better to generalize the subjective aspect of the UFO phenomenon and assume that a collective but unacknowledged fear of death is being projected on the UFOs. After the initial optimistic speculations about the visitors from space, people have recently begun to discuss their possible dangerousness and the incalculable consequences of an invasion of the earth. Grounds for an unusually intense fear of death are nowadays not far to seek: they are obvious enough, the more so as all life that is senselessly wasted and misdirected means death too. This may account for the unnatural intensification of the fear of death in our time, when life has lost its deeper meaning for so many people, forcing them to exchange the life-preserving rhythm of the aeons for the dread ticking of the clock. One would therefore wish many people the compensating attitude of the anima in our dream, and would recommend them to choose a motto like that of Hans Hopfer, a pupil of Holbein: "Death is where everything ends. I yield to none."

DREAM 5

This dream comes from a woman with an academic education. It was dreamt several years ago without reference to UFOs:

> Two women were standing on the edge of the world, seeking. The older was taller but lame. The younger was shorter and had her arm under that of the taller, as if supporting her. The older one looked out with courage (I identified her in some way with X), and the younger stood beside her with strength but feared to look. Her head was bowed (I identified myself with this second figure). Above was the crescent moon and the morning star. To the right the rising sun. An elliptical, silvery object came flying from the right. It was peopled around its rim with figures which I think were men, cloaked figures all silvery white. The women were awed and trembled in that unearthly, cosmic space, a position untenable except at the moment of vision.

After this extremely impressive dream the dreamer immediately seized a paint brush in order to fix the vision, as shown in Plate 1 (frontispiece). The dream describes a typical UFO phenomenon which, like Dream 1, contains the motif of "manning", i.e., the presence of human beings. It obviously represents a borderline situation, as the expression "on the edge of the world" shows. Out beyond is cosmic space with its planets and suns; or the beyond may be the land of the dead or the unconscious. The first possibility suggests a spaceship, the technical achievement of more highly developed planetary beings; the second, angels of some kind or departed spirits, who come to earth in order to fetch a soul. This would refer to X, who was already in need of "support", as she was ill. Her health really did give grounds for anxiety, and in fact she died about two years after the dream. Accordingly the dreamer took it as a premonition. The third possibility, that the beyond is the unconscious, points to a personification of the latter, namely the animus in his characteristic plurality; the festive white robes of the crew suggest the idea of a marital union of opposites. This symbolism, as we know, also applies to death as a final realization of wholeness. The dreamer's view that the dream gave warning of the death of her friend may therefore be right.

The dream, then, uses the symbol of a disk-like UFO manned by spirits, a spaceship that comes out of the beyond to the edge of our world in order to fetch the souls of the dead. It is not clear from the vision where the ship comes from, whether from the sun or moon or elsewhere. According to the myth in the *Acta Archelai*, it would be from the waxing moon, which increases in size according to the number of departed souls that are scooped up from the earth to the sun in twelve buckets, and from there are emptied into the moon in a purified state. The idea that the UFO might be a sort of Charon is certainly one that I have not met in the literature so far. This is hardly surprising, firstly because "classical" allusions of this sort are a rarity in people with a modern education, and secondly because they might lead to very disagreeable conclusions. The apparent increase in UFO sightings in recent years has caused disquiet in the popular mind and might easily give rise to the conclusion that, if so many spaceships appear from the beyond, a corresponding number of deaths may be expected. We know that such phenomena were interpreted like this in earlier centuries: they were portents of a "great dying", of war and pestilence, like the dark premonitions that underlie our modern fear. One ought not to assume that the great masses are so enlightened that hypotheses of this kind can no longer take root.

The Middle Ages, antiquity and prehistory have not died out, as the "enlightened" suppose, but live on merrily in large sections of the population. Mythology and magic flourish as ever in our midst and are unknown only to those whose rationalistic education has alienated them from their roots.[15] Quite apart from the ecclesiastical symbolism that embodies six thousand years of spiritual development and constantly renews itself, there are also its more disreputable relatives, magical ideas and practices which are still very much alive in spite of all education and enlightenment. One must have lived for many years in the Swiss countryside in order to become acquainted with this background, for it never appears on the surface. But once you have found the key, you stagger from one amazement to the next. Not only do you come across the primitive witch doctor in the guise of the so-called "Strudel" (wizard), you will also find blood pacts with the devil, pin-stickings and spells for drying up the milk of cattle, and regular hand-written books of magic. At the house of one of these rustic wizards I once discovered a book of this kind from the end of the 19th century, beginning with the Merseburg magic spell in modern High German and an incantation to Venus of unknown age. These wizards often have a large clientele from town and country. I myself have seen a collection of hundreds of letters of thanks which one of them received for successfully laying ghosts in houses and stables, for taking the curse off men and animals, and for curing all manner of ailments. For those of my readers who are unaware of these things and think I am exaggerating, I can point to the easily verifiable fact that the heyday of astrology was not in the benighted Middle Ages but in the middle of the 20th century, when even the newspapers do not hesitate to publish the week's

---

[15] Cf. Aniela Jaffé's *Geistererscheinungen und Vorzeichen* (Zürich, 1958), which investigates strange occurrences among modern people for their mythological content.

horoscope. A thin layer of rootless rationalists read with satisfaction in an encyclopaedia that in the year 1723 Mr. So-and-so had horoscopes cast for his children, and yet do not know that nowadays the horoscope has almost attained the rank of a visiting card. Those who have even a nodding acquaintance with this background and are in any way affected by it obey the unwritten but strictly observed convention: "One does not speak of such things". They are only whispered about, no one admits them, for no one wants to be considered all that stupid. In reality, however, it is very different.

I mention these things that infest the roots of our society chiefly on account of the symbolism of our dreams, which sounds so incomprehensible to many people because it is based on historical and contemporary facts that are unknown to them. What would they say if I connected the dream of a quite simple person with Wotan or Balder? They would accuse me of learned eccentricity, not knowing that in the same village there was a "wizard" who had taken the spell off the dreamer's stable, using for that purpose a book of magic that begins with the Merseburg incantation. Anyone who does not know that "Wotan's host"— enlightenment or no enlightenment—still roams about our Swiss cantons would accuse me of the greatest whimsicality if I referred the anxiety dream of a city dweller on a lonely Alp to the "blessed people" (the dead), when yet he is surrounded by mountainfolk for whom the "Doggeli"[16] and Wotan's nightly cavalcade are a reality which they fear without admitting it, and profess to know nothing about. It needs so little to bridge the apparent abyss that yawns between the prehistoric world and the present. Our identity with the fleeting consciousness of the present is, however, so great that we forget the "timelessness" of our psychic foundations. Everything that has lasted longer, and will last longer, than the whirligig of modern political movements is

---

[16] Swiss-German expression for the nightmare or stable spook.

regarded as fantastical nonsense that should studiously be avoided. But in that way we succumb to the greatest psychic danger that now threatens us—rootless intellectualisms which one and all reckon without their host, i.e., without the real man. Unfortunately people imagine that only the things they are conscious of affect them, and that for everything unknown there is some specialist who has long made a science out of it. This delusion is the more plausible in that nowadays it really has become impossible for an individual to assimilate the things which specialists know about and he doesn't. But since, subjectively, the most effective experiences are the most individual and therefore the most improbable, the questioner will often get no very satisfactory answer from the scientist. A typical example of this is Menzel's book on UFOs. The scientist's interest is too easily restricted to the common, the probable, the average, for that is after all the basis of every empirical science. Nevertheless a basis has little meaning unless something can be erected upon it that also leaves room for the exceptional and extraordinary.

In a borderline situation such as our dream describes we may expect something extraordinary, or rather, what seems extraordinary to us, though in reality it has always been inherent in such situations: The ship of death approaches with a corona of departed spirits, the deceased joins their company, and the multitudinous dead take the soul with them.

When archetypal ideas of this kind appear they invariably signify something unusual. It is not our interpretation that is farfetched; it is merely that the dreamer's attention, caught by the many superficial aspects of the dream, has missed the main point, namely the nearness of death, which in a sense concerns her as much as her friend. We have met the motif of the "manning" of the spaceship in the dream of the metallic spider and shall meet it again in the next one. The instinctive resistance we feel for the deeper aspect of this motif may explain why it seems to play no role in the UFO literature. We might exclaim with

Faust: "Summon not the well-known throng!" But there is no need of this summons, because the fear that hangs over the world has already taken care of that.

DREAM 6

The following dream[17] comes from California, the classic saucer country, so to speak. The dreamer is a young woman of 23.

> I was standing outside with someone (a man). It was night time and we seemed to be in a square or the centre of town—a circle. We were watching the sky. All of a sudden I saw some-thing round and fluorescent coming towards us from way in the distance. I realized it was a flying saucer. I thought it was a ridiculous joke. It got larger and larger as it came towards us. It was a huge round circle of light. Finally it covered the entire sky. It was so close, I could see figures walking back and forth on the walk round the ship. There was a railing around it. I thought someone was playing a trick, then I thought it *was* real—I looked up behind me and saw someone with a movie projector. In back of us seemed to be a building, like a hotel. These people were up high and projecting this image into the sky. I told everyone. Then I seemed to be in a sort of studio. There were two producers, competitors—both old men. I kept going from one to the other discussing my part in their pictures. There were many girls involved . . . One of the producers was direct-ing this flying-saucer thing. They were both making science fiction films and I was going to have the lead in both pictures.

The dreamer, a young film actress, was undergoing psycho-logical treatment for a marked dissociation of personality with all the accompanying symptoms. As usual, the dissociation

---

[17] I am indebted to Dr. H. Y. Kluger, Los Angeles, for this material.

expressed itself in her relations with the opposite sex, that is, in a conflict between two men who corresponded to the two incompatible halves of her personality.

COMMENTARY TO DREAM 6

As in the first two dreams, the dreamer was conscious of UFOs, and here, as there, the UFO functions as a symbol carrier. Its appearance is even expected, since the dreamer had already put herself in a "central" position for this purpose—a square or centre of the city. This gives her a central position between the opposites, equidistant from right and left, and allowing her to see or feel both sides. In the light of this "attitude" the UFO appears to be rather like an exemplification or "projection" of it. The dream insists on the projection character of the UFO, since it proves to be a cinematographic operation conducted by two rival film producers. We can easily discern in these two figures the rival objects of her dissociated love choice, and hence the underlying conflict, which should be resolved in a reconciliation of opposites. The UFO appears here in the mediating role we have met before, but it turns out to be an intentional cinematographic effect obviously lacking any reconciling significance. If we remember the important part a film producer plays in the life of a young actress, then the changing of the two rival lovers into producers suggests that the latter have acquired for her a more exalted rank or an increase in prestige. They have, so to speak, moved into the limelight of her own drama, whereas the UFO is very much dimmed, if it has not lost its significance altogether as a mere trick. The accent has gone over entirely to the producers; the apparently cosmic phenomenon is nothing more than a meaningless trick staged by them, and the dreamer's interest turns wholly to her professional ambitions. This seals the outcome of the solution offered by the dream.

It is not easy to see why the dream brings in the UFO at all, only to dispose of it in this disappointing way. In view of the suggestive circumstances at the beginning of the dream—centre and circular square—and the sensational significance of UFOs, obviously well known to the dreamer, this dénouement is rather unexpected. It is as though the dream wanted to say: "It is not like that at all—on the contrary. It is only a film trick, a bit of science fiction. Think, rather, that you have the chief role in the two pictures."

From this we can see what was the role intended for the UFO and why it had to disappear from the scene. The personality of the dreamer takes up a central position on the stage, one that compensates the splitting into opposites and is therefore a means of overcoming the dissociation. For this a powerful affect is needed in order to enforce a consistent attitude. In the affect the pendulum movement of autonomous opposites ceases and a uniform state is produced. This is accomplished by the exciting appearance of the UFO, which for a moment attracts all attention to itself.

It is clear that the UFO phenomenon in this dream is unreal and only a means to an end, as though one called out to a person "Look out!" That is why it is immediately devalued: it is not a genuine phenomenon at all, but a trick, and the dream action now proceeds to the personal problem of the dreamer and her conflict between two men. If this well-known and very common situation means more and lasts longer than a passing uncertainty of choice, this is usually due to the fact that the problem is not taken seriously—like Buridan's ass, which could not decide which of two bundles of hay it wanted to eat first. It was an artificial problem: in reality he was not hungry. This seems to be the case with our dreamer: she means neither the one nor the other, but herself. What she really wants is told her by the dream, which changes the lovers into producers, represents the situation as a film project, and gives her the chief role in the pictures. That is what the dreamer really intends: in the interests of her profession she wants to play the chief role, that of the young lover, regardless of any partner. But evidently she cannot quite bring it off in reality, because she is still tempted to regard her partners as real, when in fact they are only playing a role in her own drama. This does not speak very well for her artistic vocation, and she is right to feel some doubt as to its seriousness for her. In contradistinction to her vacillating conscious attitude, the dream points decidedly to her profession as her true love and thus gives her the solution to her conflict.

Any insight into the nature of the UFO phenomenon is not to be expected from this dream. The UFO is used only as a sort of alarm signal, thanks to the collective excitement occasioned by flying saucers. Interesting or alarming as the phenomenon may be, young people have, or claim, the right to regard the problem of "her and him" as much more fascinating. In this case the young woman was certainly right, for when one is still in the process of development the earth and its laws are of more significance than that message resounding from afar, which the signs in heaven proclaim. Since youth lasts for a very long time and its peculiar state of mind is the highest that many human lives attain, this psychological limitation is equally true of the grey-haired, whose birthdays are nothing more than nostalgic celebrations of their twentieth. At best the outcome is concentration on one's profession, any further development being regarded as a mere disturbance. Neither age nor position nor education is any protection against this psychological standstill. Human society is after all still very young, for what are three or five thousand years on a longer view!

I have introduced this dream as a paradigm of the way the unconscious can also deal with the problem that concerns us here. I wanted to show that the symbols cannot be interpreted in a uniform manner and that their meaning depends on many different factors. Life cannot go forward except from the place where one happens to be.

In the next section I shall discuss some pictures relating to UFOs. The painter of "The Fire Sower", to whom I had written that certain details seemed to be connected with the strange apparitions in the skies, sent me the following dream, which he had on September 12th 1957.

DREAM 7

I found myself, together with other people, on the top of a hill, looking out over a beautiful, broad, undulating landscape teeming with lush verdure.

Suddenly a flying saucer floated into view, paused at eye-level before us and lay there, clear and shining, in the sunlight. It did not look like a machine but like a deep-sea fish, round and flat, but enormously big (about 30 to 40 feet in diameter). It was speckled all over with blue, grey, and white spots. Its edges undulated and quivered all the time; they acted as oars and rudders.

This creature began circling round us, then all at once, as though fired from a cannon, shot straight up into the blue sky, came rushing down again with inconceivable speed, and once more circled round our hill. It was obviously doing this for our benefit. (Once when it flew quite close, it seemed to be much smaller and looked like a hammer-headed shark.)

Now it had somehow landed in our vicinity . . . An occupant got out and came straight towards me. (A semi-human woman?) The other people fled and waited at a respectful distance, looking back at us.

The woman told me that they knew me well in that other world (from which she had come) and were watching how I fulfilled my task (mission?). She spoke in a stern, almost threatening tone and seemed to attach great importance to the charge laid upon me.

COMMENTARY TO DREAM 7

The occasion for the dream was the anticipation of a visit which the dreamer intended to pay me during the next few days. The exposition shows a positive, hopeful feeling of expectancy. The dramatic development begins with the sudden appearance of a UFO, which has the obvious intention of showing itself as clearly as possible to the observer. On closer inspection he sees that it is not a machine but an animal of sorts, a deep-sea fish, something like a giant ray, which, as we know, sometimes makes attempts to fly. Its movements emphasize the relationship of the UFO to the observers. These overtures lead to a landing. A semi-human figure climbs out of the UFO, thus revealing an intelligent human relationship between the UFO and its observers. This impression is strengthened by the fact that it is a feminine figure which, because it is unknown and indefinite, belongs to the anima type. The numinosity of this archetype causes a panic reaction among the "people" present—in other words, the dreamer registers a subjective reaction of flight. The reason for this lies in the fateful significance of the anima figure: she is the Sphinx of Oedipus, a Cassandra, the messenger of the Grail, the "white lady" who gives warning of death, etc. This view is borne out by the message she conveys: she comes from another world where the dreamer is known, and where they watch attentively how he fulfils his "mission".

The anima personifies the collective unconscious,[18] the "realm of the Mothers", which, as experience shows, has a distinct tendency to influence the conscious conduct of life and, when this is not possible, to erupt violently into consciousness in order to confront it with strange and seemingly incomprehensible contents. The UFO in the dream is a content of this kind whose strangeness leaves nothing to be desired. The difficulty of

[18] When the shadow, the inferior personality, is in large measure unconscious, the unconscious is represented by a masculine figure.

integration is in this case so great that the dreamer's ordinary powers of comprehension fail him and he resorts to mythical means of explanation—star dwellers, angels, spirits, gods—even before he knows what he has seen. So great is the numinosity of these ideas that one never asks oneself whether it might not be a subjective perception of collective unconscious processes. For in the common estimation a subjective observation can only be either "true" or else, as a delusion of the senses or a hallucination, it can only be "untrue". The fact that the latter are also true phenomena with sufficient reasons of their own is apparently never taken into account, so long as no obviously pathological disturbance is present. There are, however, manifestations of the unconscious, even in normal people, which can be so "real" and impressive that the observer instinctively resists taking his perception as a delusion or hallucination. His instinct is right: when an inner process cannot be integrated it is often projected outwards. It is, indeed, the rule that a man's consciousness projects all perceptions coming from the feminine personification of the unconscious on to an anima figure, i.e., a real woman, to whom he is as much bound as he is in reality to the contents of the unconscious. This explains the fateful quality of the anima, which is also suggested in the dream by her question: How are you fulfilling your life's task ("mission"), your raison d'être, the meaning and purpose of your existence? This is the question of individuation, the most fateful of all questions, which was put to Oedipus in the form of the childish riddle of the Sphinx and was radically misunderstood by him. (Can one imagine an intelligent Athenian playgoer ever being taken in by the "terrible riddles" of the Sphinx?) Oedipus did not use his intelligence to see through the uncanny nature of this childishly simple and all too facile riddle, and therefore fell victim to his tragic fate, because he thought he had answered the question. It was the Sphinx itself that he ought to have answered and not its façade.

Just as Mephistopheles proves to be the "quintessence of the poodle", so the anima is the quintessence of the UFO. But Mephistopheles is not the whole of *Faust*, and the anima too is only a part of the whole, which is obscurely alluded to in the deep-sea fish, the "rotundum". Here the anima plays the role of the mediatrix between the unconscious and the conscious, a dual figure like the Sphinx, compounded of animal instinct (body) and specifically human qualities (head). In her body lie the forces that determine man's fate, in her head the power to modify them intelligently. (This basic idea is also reflected in the picture we shall reproduce later.) At this point the dream speaks a mythical language that makes use of conceptions of another world and of angelic beings who watch the doings of men. This vividly expresses the symbiosis of conscious and unconscious.

Such, at any rate, would seem to be the nearest we can get to a satisfactory explanation. With regard to the possible metaphysical background we must honestly confess our ignorance and the impossibility of proof. The unmistakable tendency of the dream is the attempt to create a psychologem which we meet again and again in this and many other forms, regardless of whether the UFOs should be understood as concrete realities or as subjective phenomena. The psychologem is a reality in its own right. It is based on a real perception which has no need of the physical reality of UFOs, because it manifested itself long before UFOs were ever heard of.

The end of the dream lays special weight on the woman's message, emphasizing its seriousness, even its menacing quality. The collective parallel to this is the widespread fear that the UFOs may not be harmless after all, and that communication with other planets might have unpredictable consequences. This view is supported by the fact that the suppression of certain information by the American authorities[19] cannot be relegated entirely to the realm of fable.

[19] Cf. Keyhoe, *The Flying Saucer Conspiracy*.

The seriousness, indeed dangerousness, of the problem of individuation cannot be denied in an age in which the destructive effects of mass-mindedness are so clearly apparent, for individuation is the great alternative that faces our western civilization. It is a fact that in a dictator State the individual is robbed of his freedom, and that we too are threatened by this political development and are not at all sure of the right means of defence. Hence the question arises in all urgency: are we going to let ourselves be robbed of our individual freedom, and what can we do to stop it?

Anxiously we look round for collective measures, thereby reinforcing the very mass-mindedness we want to fight against. There is only one remedy for the levelling effect of all collective measures, and that is to emphasize and increase the value of the individual. A fundamental change of attitude (*metanoia*) is required, a real recognition of the whole man. This can only be the business of the individual and it must begin with the individual in order to be real. This is the message of our dream, a message addressed to the dreamer from the collective, instinctual foundations of humanity. Large political and social organizations must not be ends in themselves, but merely temporary expedients. Just as it was felt necessary in America to break up the great Trusts, so the destruction of huge organizations will eventually prove to be a necessity because, like a cancerous growth, they eat away man's nature as soon as they become ends in themselves and attain autonomy. From that moment they grow beyond man and escape his control. He becomes their victim and is sacrificed to the madness of an idea that knows no master. All great organizations in which the individual no longer counts are exposed to this danger. There seems to be only one way of countering this threat to our lives, and that is the "revaluation" of the individual.

So vitally important a measure cannot, however, be put into effect at will, that is, by planning and insight, because the individual human being is too small and weak. What is needed, rather, is an involuntary faith, a kind of metaphysical command, which no one can manufacture artificially, with his own will and understanding. It can only come about spontaneously. One such dominant underlies our dream. My suggestion that certain details of the picture might be connected with the UFO problem was sufficient to constellate in the dreamer the archetype underlying this collective phenomenon and to give him a numinous insight into the metaphysical significance of the individual. The empirical man extends beyond his conscious boundaries, his life and fate have far more than a personal meaning. He attracts the interest of "another world"; achievements are expected of him which go beyond the empirical realm and its narrow limits. The status of the individual is enhanced, and he acquires a cosmic importance. This numinous transformation is not the result of conscious intention or intellectual conviction, but is brought about by the impact of overwhelming archetypal impressions.

An experience of this kind is not without its dangers, because it often has an inflating effect on the individual. His ego fancies itself increased and exalted, whereas in reality it is thrust into the background. In fact, the ego almost needs an inflation (the feeling of being one of the elect, for instance) in order not to lose the ground from under its feet, although it is precisely the inflation that lifts it off its foundations. It is not the ego that is exalted; rather, something greater than it makes its appearance: the self, a symbol that expresses the whole man. But the ego loves to think itself the whole man and therefore has the greatest difficulty in avoiding the danger of inflation. This is another reason why such experiences are shunned, indeed feared as pathological, and why the very idea of the unconscious and any preoccupation with it is unwelcome. It was not so long ago that we were living in a primitive state of mind with its "perils of the soul"—loss of soul, states of possession, etc., which threatened the unity of the personality, that is, the ego. These dangers are still a long way from having been overcome in our civilized society. Though they no longer afflict the individual to the same degree, this is certainly not true of social or national groups on a large scale, as contemporary history shows only too clearly. They are psychic epidemics that destroy the individual.

In face of this danger the only thing that helps is for the individual to be seized by a powerful emotion which, instead of suppressing or destroying him, makes him whole. This can only happen when the unconscious man is added to the conscious one. The process of unification is only partly under the control of our will; for the rest it happens involuntarily. With the conscious mind we are able, at most, to get within reach of the unconscious process, and must then wait and see what will happen next. From the conscious standpoint the whole process looks like an adventure or a "quest", somewhat in the manner of Bunyan's *Pilgrim's Progress*. Esther Harding, in a detailed study,[20] has shown that in spite of the differences of language and outlook Bunyan was speaking of the same inward experiences which also befall people today when they choose the "strait and narrow" path. I would recommend her book to anyone who wants to know what the individuation process really is. To the constantly reiterated question "What can I do?" I know no other answer except "Become what you have always been", namely, the wholeness which we have lost in the midst of our civilized, conscious existence, a wholeness which we always were without knowing it. Esther Harding's book speaks such a simple and universal language that any man of good will, even though he lack specialized knowledge, can get an idea of what it is all about. He will also understand why, despite the fact that his question, "What on earth can I do in the present threatening world situation, with my feeble powers?" seems so important to him, it were better for him to do nothing and to leave things as they are. To worship collective ideals and work with the big

---

[20] *Journey into the Self*, New York, 1956.

organizations is spectacularly meritorious, but they nevertheless dig the grave for the individual. A group is always of less value than the average run of its members, and when the group consists in the main of shirkers and good-for-nothings, what then? Then the ideals it preaches count for nothing too. Also, the right means in the hands of the wrong man work the wrong way, as a Chinese proverb informs us.

The message which the UFO brings to the dreamer is a time problem that concerns us all. The signs appear in the heavens so that everyone shall see them. They bid each of us remember his own soul and his own wholeness, because this is the answer the West should give to the danger of mass-mindedness.

3

UFOS IN MODERN PAINTING

Whilst I was collecting the material for this essay, I happened to come across the work of a painter who, profoundly disturbed by the way things are going in the world today, has given expression to the fundamental fear of our age—the catastrophic outbreak of destructive forces which everyone dreads. It is, indeed, a law of painting to give visible shape to the dominant trends of the age, and for some time now painters have taken as their subject the disintegration of forms and the "breaking of tables", creating pictures which, abstractly detached from meaning and feeling alike, are distinguished by their "meaninglessness" as much as by their deliberate aloofness from the spectator. These painters have immersed themselves in the destructive element and have created a new conception of beauty, one that delights in the alienation of meaning and of feeling. Everything consists of debris, unorganized fragments, holes, distortions, overlappings, infantilisms and crudities which outdo the clumsiest attempts of primitive art and belie the traditional idea of skill. Just as women's fashions find every innovation, however absurd and repellent, "beautiful", so too does modern art of this kind. It is the "beauty" of chaos. That is what this art heralds and eulogizes: the gorgeous rubbish heap of our civilization. It must be admitted that such an undertaking is productive of fear, especially when allied to the political possibilities of our catastrophic age. One can well imagine that in an epoch of the "great destroyers" it is a particular satisfaction to be at least the broom that sweeps the rubbish into the corner.

The painter of Plate 2 has summoned up the courage to admit the existence of a deep-rooted and universal fear and express it in his art, just as other artists have dared—or were driven—to choose as their motif the conscious and unconscious will for destruction and to depict the collapse of our civilization in chaos. They did this with a passionate superiority worthy of

Plate 2 The Fire Sower

Herostratus,[1] with no fear of the consequences. Fear, however, is an admission of inferiority; it shrinks back from chaos and longs for solid, tangible reality, for the continuity of what has been, for meaning and purpose—in a word, for civilization. It is conscious that all destruction is the result of inadequacy, and that we lack something vital which could halt the onrush of chaos. It must counter the fragmentariness of our world by a striving to be healed and made whole. But since this apparently cannot be found in the present, we cannot even conceive what would make us whole. We have become sceptical, and chimerical ideas of world improvement stand low in the list. The old panaceas that have finally failed are no longer trusted, or only half-heartedly. The lack of any serviceable or even credible ruling ideas has created a situation that resembles a *tabula rasa*—almost anything might appear. The phenomenon of the UFOs may well be just such an apparition.

More or less conscious of the analogy with a UFO, the artist[2] has painted a round, fiery object rotating in the heavens above the darkening city. Following a naïve impulse to personification, he has given it the suggestion of a face, so that it became a head separated from the body to which it belongs. Like the head, the body consists of flame. It is the gigantic figure of a spectral "sower, who went forth to sow". He sows flames, and instead of water fire falls from heaven. It seems to be an invisible fire, a "fire of the Philosophers",[3] for the city takes no notice of it, nor does it start a conflagration. It falls unheeded, apparently to no purpose, like seed from the hand of the sower. Like an immaterial

---

[1] Herostratus, in order to make his name immortal, burned down the temple of Artemis in Ephesus, 365 B.C.

[2] He was not a saucer addict and had not read the UFO literature.

[3] In what follows there are a number of allusions to medieval symbolism, which may perhaps be unknown to the reader. He will find the necessary documentation in my book *Psychology and Alchemy*.

essence the fiery figure strides through the houses of the city—
two worlds which interpenetrate yet do not touch.

As the "Philosophers", that is, the old masters of alchemy,
assure us, their "water" is at the same time "fire". Their Mercurius is *hermaphroditus* and *duplex*, a *complexio oppositorum*, the messenger of the gods, the One and All. He is moreover a Hermes
katachthonios (subterranean Mercurius), a spirit emanating from
the earth, shining bright and burning hot, heavier than metal
and lighter than air, serpent and eagle at once, poisonous and
alexipharmic. He is the panacea itself and the elixir of life, but on
the other hand he is a deadly danger for the ignorant. For the
educated person of those days, who studied the philosophy of
alchemy as part of his general equipment—it was a real *religio
medici*—this figure of the Fire Sower would have been full of
allusions, and he would have had no difficulty in assimilating it
to his stock of knowledge. For us, however, it is a disconcerting
oddity, and we look round in vain for anything to compare it
with, because what the conscious mind thinks is so utterly
different from what the unconscious is aiming at. The picture
illustrates the incommensurable nature of two worlds which
interpenetrate but do not touch. One could compare it to a
dream that is trying to tell the dreamer that his consciousness
lives in a dully rational world while all the time he is confronted
with the nocturnal phantom of a *homo maximus*. Understood as a
subjective reflex, the giant figure could be taken as a kind of
psychological spectre of the Brocken. In that case one would
have to posit a repressed megalomania of which the artist himself is afraid. The whole thing would then be shifted on to a
pathological plane and would be nothing more than a neurotic
self-confession slyly insinuated into the picture. The frightening
spectacle of an apocalyptic world situation would be reduced to
the personal, egocentric fear which everyone feels who nurses a
secret megalomania—the fear that one's imagined grandeur will
come to grief on colliding with reality. The tragedy of the world

would be turned into the comedy of a little cock of the dung-hill. We know only too well that such jokes occur all too frequently.

So facile an argument is not sufficient to make this descent from the sublime to the ridiculous appear at all plausible. The significance of the figure lies not so much in its size and strangeness as in the numinosity of its unconscious symbolical background. If it were no more than a matter of personal vanity and infantile self-assertion, the choice of a different symbol would have been far more appropriate—the figure of a successful and envied rival in one's own profession, for instance, or one that increased the artist's status. But here everything points to the contrary: the figure is in every respect archetypal. It is of super-human stature, like an archaic king or a god; it consists not of flesh and bone, but of fire; its head is round, like a luminary, or like the angel's in Revelation 10: 1: "and a rainbow was upon his head, and his face was as it were the sun, and his feet as pillars of fire", or like the starry heads of the planetary gods in medieval paintings. The head is separated from the body, as if to emphasize its independence, and could be compared to the arcane substance of the alchemists, the philosophical gold, the *aurum non vulgi*, the "head"-element or "omega"-element, a symbol that originated with Zosimos of Panopolis (third century A.D.). The spirit is a wanderer who roams over the earth, sowing fiery grains, like those gods and god-men who wander about and do miracles, whether of destruction or of healing. Psalm 104: 4 likens God's "ministers" to a "flaming fire"; God himself is a "consuming fire". "Fire" signifies the intensity of affect and is the symbol of the Holy Ghost, who came down in the form of tongues of fire.

The characteristics of this fire-sowing figure are all steeped in tradition, some of them conscious and biblical, some of them derived from the inherited predisposition to reproduce similar but autochthonous ideas. The artist's more or less conscious allusion to the UFO phenomenon throws light on the inner relationship between the two sets of ideas: the one interprets the other, because they both spring from the same source. Another picture by the same artist shows a motif in blue and white similar to that of Dream 2. A spring landscape, the blue sky arching above it, softened by silvery vapours. At one point the thin veil of cloud is pierced by a round opening, through which you can see the deep blue of the heavens. To either side of the opening there is a wedge of white cloud, so that the whole looks like an eye. Extremely realistic automobiles rush along on the road below. "They do not see it", the artist explained to me. In this picture the UFO is replaced by the traditional eye of God, gazing from heaven.

These symbolical ideas are archetypal images that are not derived from recent UFO sightings but always existed. There are historical reports of the same kind from earlier decades and centuries. Thirty years ago, before Flying Saucers were heard of, I myself came across very similar dream-visions, for instance a multitude of little suns or gold coins falling from the sky, or the figure of a boy whose clothes were made of shining golden circles, or a wanderer in a field of stars, or the rising of a sun-like object which in the course of the visions developed into a mandala. I also remember a picture that was shown to me in 1919, of a town stretching along the edge of the sea, an ordinary modern port with smoking factory chimneys, fortifications, soldiers, etc. Above it there lay a thick bank of cloud, and above this there rolled an "austere image",[4] a shining disk divided into quadrants by a cross. Here again we have two worlds separated by a bank of cloud and not touching.

From the very beginning the UFO reports interested me as being, very possibly, symbolical rumours, and since 1947 I have collected all the books I could get hold of on the subject. UFOs

[4] Cf. *Psychology and Alchemy*, p. 148.

seemed to me to have a good deal in common with mandala symbolism, about which I first wrote in 1927, in *The Secret of the Golden Flower*. Though one would like to give honest eye-witnesses and radar experts the benefit of the doubt, it must nevertheless be stressed that there is an unmistakable resemblance between the UFO phenomena and certain psychic conditions which should not be overlooked in evaluating the observations. Besides affording a possible psychological explanation the comparison sheds light on the psychic compensation of the collective fear weighing on our hearts. The meaning of the rumour is not exhausted by its being explained as a causal symptom; rather, it has the value and significance of a living symbol, i.e., a dynamic factor which, because of the general ignorance and lack of understanding, has to confine itself to producing a visionary rumour. The fact that there is a numinous quality about all archetypal products is responsible not only for the spread of the rumour but also for its persistence. The numinosity of the complex has the further result that it stimulates deeper reflection and more careful research, until finally someone asks: What is the meaning of such a rumour at the present time? What future developments are being prepared in the unconscious of modern man? Long before Pallas Athene sprang, fully armed, from the head of All-Father Zeus, anticipatory and preparatory dreams had revolved round this theme and transmitted abortive sketches of it to the conscious mind. It depends on us whether we help coming events to birth by understanding them, and reinforce their healing effect, or whether we repress them with our prejudices, narrow-mindedness and ignorance, thus turning their effect into its opposite, into poison and destruction.

This brings me to a question I have been asked over and over again by my patients: What is the use of a compensation that, because of its symbolic form, is not understood by the conscious mind? Apart from those not so uncommon cases where only a little reflection is needed to understand the meaning of a dream, we can take it as a general rule that the compensation is not immediately obvious and is therefore easily overlooked. The language of the unconscious does not have the intentional clarity of conscious language; it is a condensation of numerous data, many of them subliminal, whose connection with conscious contents is unknown. These data do not take the form of a directed judgment, but follow an instinctive, archaic "pattern" which, because of its mythological character, is not recognized by the reasoning mind. The reaction of the unconscious is a natural phenomenon that is not concerned to benefit or guide the personal human being, but is regulated exclusively by the demands of psychic equilibrium. Thus there are times when, as I have often seen, a dream that is not understood can have a compensatory effect, even though as a rule conscious understanding is indispensable, on the alchemical principle "*Quod natura relinquit imperfectum, ars perficit*" (what nature leaves imperfect is perfected by the art). Were this not so, human reflection and effort would be superfluous. For its part the conscious mind often proves incapable of recognizing the full scope and significance of certain vital situations it has created for itself, and so challenges the unconscious to bring up the subliminal context, which however is written not in rational language but in an archaic one with two or more meanings. And since the metaphors it uses reach far back into the history of the human mind, its interpreters will need historical knowledge in order to understand its meaning.

This is also true of our painting: it is a picture that reveals its meaning only with the aid of historical amplification. The fear from which it sprang is explained by the collision of the artist's conscious world with a strange apparition that came from an unknown region of his being. This world behind, below, and above us appears to us as the unconscious, which adds its subliminal contents to the images we consciously create. Thus there arises the figure of a *homo maximus*, an Anthropos and *filius hominis* of fiery nature, whose godlikeness or numinosity is proved by the fact that he immediately evokes similar figures in our minds, such as Enoch, Christ,[5] or Elijah, or the visions of Daniel and Ezekiel. Since Yahweh's fire chastises, kills and consumes, the spectator is also at liberty to think of Jacob Boehme's "wrath-fire", which contains hell itself, together with Lucifer. The scattered flames could therefore signify the "enthusiasm" of the Holy Ghost as well as the fire of evil passions—in other words, the extremes of emotion and affect which human nature is capable of, but which in ordinary life are prohibited, suppressed, hidden, or altogether unconscious. It is probably not without good reason that the name "Lucifer" applies to both Christ and the devil. The Temptation in Matthew 4: 3ff. describes the split between them, and the fight against the devil and his angels exemplifies the mutual opposition and at the same time the inner relationship between the two sides of a moral judgment. An opposition exists only where two principles conflict with one another, but not where one is and the other not, or where there is only a one-sided dependence, such as when only good has substance but not evil.

The fiery figure is ambiguous and therefore unites the opposites. It is a "uniting symbol", a totality beyond human consciousness, making whole the fragmentariness of the merely conscious man. It is a bringer of salvation and disaster at once. What it will be, for good or ill, depends on the understanding and ethical decision of the individual. The picture is a kind of message to modern man, admonishing him to meditate on the signs that appear in the heavens and to interpret them aright.

The reflection of the UFO phenomenon in the artist's imagination has produced a picture whose basic features are similar to those already discussed in the dreams. It belongs to

---

[5] "I am come to send fire on earth, and what will I, if it be already kindled?" Luke 12: 49.

another dimension, to a world of gods that seems to have no connection with our reality. The picture gives one the impression of a vision, beheld by one singled out and elect, who was permitted to see what the gods do secretly on earth. The artist's interpretation of the phenomenon is at an astronomical remove from the popular view that UFOs are controlled space machines.

PLATE 3: THE FOURTH DIMENSION

Like the previous painting, this too is contemporary. In order to avoid misunderstandings I must point out at once that it is painted on canvas and that the peculiar treatment of the background is not the result of the grain of wood showing through. It was the artist's intention to represent something growing or flowing. Similarly, he uses the skyline of a city to emphasize a horizontal plane cutting through the picture. Whereas Jakoby contrasts the low-lying city with the spacious night sky, Birkhäuser has moved the horizontal upward, to indicate that the essence of the background also flows downwards through the depths of the earth. The colour of the city is a soft dark red; the background is a light, watery, greenish blue streaked with pale yellow and vermilion.

In this background there are fourteen more or less distinct circles. Ten of them form the eyes of shadowy faces, half animal, half human. The other four look like knots in wood or like dark objects floating about with haloes round them. From the mouth of the large face at the top there issues a stream of water that flows downwards through the city. Neither touches the other: two incommensurable events are taking place on two totally different planes, one vertical, the other horizontal. Since, on the horizontal plane, there is a three-dimensional city bathed in a light that shines from the left of the picture and has nothing to do with the background, this background can only be

Plate 3 The Fourth Dimension

considered as a *fourth dimension*. The intersecting lines of the two worlds form a cross (city and waterfall). The only discernible connection between the two is the downward glance of the eyes in the large face upon the city. The pronounced nostrils and abnormally wide-apart eyes show that the face is only partly human. Of the four other faces, the only unmistakably human one is on the top left. The face on the bottom left can only be made out very faintly. If we regard the face in the middle, distinguished both by its size and by the fact that the water flows from its mouth, as the main face and as the source, then the ground structure of the picture is a quincunx:

$$\oplus \quad + $$
$$+$$
$$+ \quad +$$

This is a symbol of the *quinta essentia*, which is identical with the Philosophers' Stone. It is the circle divided into four with the centre, or the divinity extended in four directions, or the four functions of consciousness with their unitary substrate, the self. Here the quaternity has a 3 + 1 structure: three animal-daemonic faces and one human one. This peculiar feature of our picture recalls the quaternity discussed by Plato in the Timaeus and experienced still earlier by Ezekiel in his vision of the four seraphim. One of them had a human face, the other three had animal faces. The motif appears again in certain representations of the sons of Horus and in the emblems of the evangelists, as well as in the four gospels (three synoptic, one "Gnostic") and in the four Persons of Christian metaphysics: the Trinity and the devil. The 3 + 1 structure is a motif that runs all through alchemy and was attributed to Maria the Copt or Jewess. Goethe took it up again in the Cabiri scene in *Faust*. The number 4 as the natural division of the circle is a symbol of wholeness in alchemical philosophy, and it should not be forgotten that the central

Christian symbol is a quaternity too, which, in the form of the long cross, even has the 3 + 1 structure.[6]

This painting, like the previous one, depicts the collision of two incommensurable worlds, vertical and horizontal, which meet only at one point: in the Sower's intention to scatter fire on the earth, and in the downward glance of the eyes.

Coming now to the four circles[7] which are not eyes, we note that only one of them—on the extreme left—is completely round and solid-looking. The circle on the right of the mouth is light with a dark centre; a third circle appears to be emitting a whitish vapour; a fourth circle is half hidden by the flowing water. They form a differentiated quaternity in contrast to the undifferentiated ogdoad of eyes, which, if we disregard the main face, belong to a quaternity with a 3 + 1 structure.

It is difficult to say how much in the main face is animal and how much is human. But since it represents the "source of living water" (quintessence, *aurum potabile*, *aqua permanens*, *vinum ardens*, *elixir vitae*, etc.) and appears to have an animal component, its doubtfully human character is plain enough. One thinks of the figure "having the likeness of a human form" who appeared above the sapphire throne in Ezekiel's vision, and of Yahweh's wildness, which so often breaks through in the Old Testament. In Christian iconography the Trinity consists of three human persons (occasionally depicted as a tricephalus), while the fourth, the devil, is traditionally represented as half-animal. Our mandala seems to be complementary to the Christian totality.

---

[6] In H. G. Wells the "time machine" seems to have three visible rods, but the fourth "has an odd, twinkling appearance, as if it were not real".

[7] In this connection I would like to draw attention to van Gogh's *Starry Night* (1889). There the stars are painted as large shining disks, though the eye never sees them like that. Speaking of his picture, van Gogh uses the expression "pantheistic frenzy", calling it the "remnant of an apocalyptic fantasy" and comparing the starry disks to a "group of living figures who are like one of us". The painting is supposed to be derived from a dream.

One further fact deserves notice: the two lower faces, though inverted, are not reflections of the two upper ones, but are independent entities representing a lower as opposed to an upper world. Moreover, one of the two upper faces is light, the other considerably darker, with pointed ears. In contrast to this opposition the water flows uniformly from above downwards, thus forming a potential. The source lies not only above the earthly horizontal but also above the middle line of the picture, so that the upper world is characterized as the source of life. Since the three-dimensional human body is ordinarily thought of as the seat of life and strength, this is compensated by placing the source in the fourth dimension. It flows from an ideal centre. The fourth dimension is therefore only apparently symmetrical, in reality it is asymmetrical—a problem that is of importance both to nuclear physics and to the psychology of the unconscious.

The "four-dimensional" background is a "vision", in the dual sense of seeing and of something seen. It seems to be a matter of pure chance that it has turned out so and not otherwise, when the merest accident could have given it a quite different appearance. The sight of these round blobs aimlessly scattered over a wishy-washy surface, most of them serving for eyes in indistinct animal-human faces lacking any definite expression, fails to arouse our interest. The picture discourages any attempt to find access to it, for the chance products of nature, if they lack aesthetic charm, have no effect on our sensibilities. Their chance-fulness makes the slightest attempt to interpret them seem like empty speculation. It needs the interest of the psychologist, so often incomprehensible to the layman, to follow up a vague instinct for order, using for this purpose the most primitive of all devices, namely numbers. When there are few or no characteristics that can be compared with one another, number remains as the ordering schema. Nevertheless, the little disks or holes are distinctly round and the majority of them are eyes. It is only by chance—I must repeat this—that numbers and other patterns appear whose exact repetition would be extremely improbable. In such cases we must refrain from all statistical or experimental thinking, for a probability test of this picture would involve astronomical figures. Investigations of this kind are only possible when a very simple experiment can be repeated over and over again in the shortest time, like Rhine's tests. Our picture is a unique and complex occurrence which from the statistical point of view is entirely meaningless. But from the psychological point of view such curiosities may be meaningful, because the conscious mind is involuntarily impressed by their numinosity. We must therefore take account of them, however improbable and irrational they may appear to be, just because they are important factors in a psychological process. But I must emphasize that nothing will have been proved.

Since psychology touches man on the practical side, it cannot be satisfied with averages, because these only give information about his general behaviour. Instead, it has to turn its attention to the individual exceptions, which are murdered by statistics. The human soul attains its true meaning not in the average but in the unique, and this does not count in a scientific procedure. Rhine's experiments have taught us, if practical experience has not already done so, that the improbable does occur, and that our picture of the world only tallies with reality when the improbable has a place in it. This point of view is anathema to the exclusively scientific attitude, despite the fact that without exceptions there would be no statistics at all. Moreover, in actual reality the exceptions are almost more important than the rule.

This picture allows some conclusions to be drawn as to the nature of the objects appearing in the sky. The "sky" is not the blue vault we see, nor is it the star-filled universe; it is a strange fourth dimension containing supernatural beings as well as dark disks or round holes. If they are holes, then modern physics suggests that they may be three-dimensional bodies lacking a fourth dimension. The background has a fluid, watery character in striking contrast to the exclusively fiery nature of the previous picture. Fire symbolizes dynamism, passion, and emotion, whereas water with its coolness and substantiality represents the passive object, detached contemplation, hence the thirst-quenching *aqua doctrinae* and the *refrigerium*[8] that puts out the fire, like the salamander of alchemy.

As the old masters say: "Our water is fire"—an identity which, as soon as we think about it, splits into opposites, like the unconscious God-image. This seeming mystery is characteristic of all that is: it is so and yet not so, especially the unconscious, whose reality we can experience only in parables. In the same way a fourth dimension can be regarded only as a mathematical fiction, an intellectual sophistry, or a revelation of the unconscious, for we have no direct experience of it.

The unconscious arrangement of the elements composing the picture therefore suggests that the UFOs are subliminal contents that have become visible; that they are, in a word, archetypal figures.

PLATE 4: PAINTING BY YVES TANGUY

The painting by Yves Tanguy dates from the year 1927, thus anticipating by more than a decade the great bombings of cities. For this is what the picture brings to mind. As a contemporary painting is usually rather difficult to interpret, because its whole aim is to abolish meaning and form and replace them by something strange, I have followed the method of showing it to as many different people as possible, in this way conducting a kind of Rorschach test. Most of them took the black and white background, which combines a minimum of intelligibility with a

---

[8] The refreshing, cool water of life in paradise after the heat of purgatory.

Plate 4 Painting by Yves Tanguy

maximum of abstraction, to be a plane surface. This is supported by the fact that the light causes the five central forms to cast shadows. It can be seen that these shadows fall on a plane. The interpretation of this varies considerably: some thought it was a sea covered with drift ice in the Polar night, others a sea of fog at night time, others the bleak surface of a distant planet like Uranus or Neptune, and others a great city illuminated at night, situated along the edge of bays, like San Francisco or New York. The strange quincunx suspended over the "city" left most of them puzzled. Some interpreted it at once as falling bombs and explosions. The form in the middle was taken to be a sea creature (sea anemone, octopus, etc.) or a flower, or else a daemonic face with tangled hair (looking down to the left); others saw it as the swirling smoke of a great fire. The four figures surrounding it were understood as sea animals, puffs of smoke, fungi or, because of the horns, as devils. The one on the top left, whose vivid yellowish-green contrasts with the dull, indeterminate tones of the others, was interpreted as poisonous smoke, a water-plant, flame, a house on fire, etc. I must admit that for me the comparison with a city at night by the sea, viewed from a considerable height as from an aeroplane, was the most convincing.

The horizon is lost in cloudy forms over which hangs a faint circular luminosity; to the left of this is a dimly lit cloud bank (?), shaped like a cigar. In the centre of the brightness there is, as if by accident, a barely visible spot of the same colour as the yellowish-green "flame" (top left of the quincunx). A similar, but clearly visible, spot can be seen further down (centre right), directly above the city. A faint line connects it with another yellowish-green spot, apparently a continuation of the flame. The longish second spot points towards the centre of faintly discernible concentric circles that suggest rotation. It is interesting to note that the first-mentioned spot at the top of the picture is also connected with concentric circles. Unfortunately they cannot be seen in the photograph, because it is too dark; they appear only as a circular luminosity surrounding the yellowish spot, but can be felt to the touch as lightly raised lines. Probably they were scratched on with a pointed instrument. There can be no doubt about their circular nature, which is clearly apparent in the lower concentric formation.

These details seem to be a matter of pure chance, the impression also given by the previous picture. Their fortuitous nature cannot be denied, but they assume a rather different aspect when submitted to a comparative procedure. As if by chance two luminous whirls with dark centres, and an equally fortuitous cigar form, appear in the night sky, together with a bright spot and a line connecting the second whirl with the flame. One can easily let one's imagination run and interpret the flame as belonging to a projectile shot out of the whirl, or, as we would now say, from a UFO—for UFOs are said to have incendiary tendencies, among other things. Here it is sowing fire, as a distinct line connects it with the flame. There are, however, a number of other wavy lines crossing the picture, like highways or boundary lines. Have they anything to do with the phenomena in the sky? So much in this picture remains conjecture, for instance the indeterminable corporeal shapes, which, together with the "flame", form a quaternity with a 3 + 1 structure. The structure in the middle is equally difficult to interpret, but it is obviously of a different, more nebulous nature and is thereby distinguished from the others, though like them it throws a shadow.

The description of the picture would be incomplete if I omitted to mention an important factor which reveals itself on closer examination: the cylindrical, phallic cloud (?) is aimed straight at the topmost luminous whirl, and this could be interpreted sexualistically as cohabitation. Similarly, from the lower whirl a little flame leaps out, which is connected in turn with the big flame on the left. The latter, in psychological terms, is the One differentiated from the Three, the one differentiated function contrasted with the three undifferentiated functions, and hence the main function (or, alternatively, the inferior function). The four together form an unfolded totality symbol, the self in its empirical aspect. The name of one of the Gnostic deities is Barbelo, "god is four". According to an early Christian idea the unity of the incarnate God rests on the four pillars of the gospels (representing the 3 + 1 structure), just as the Gnostic *monogenes* (*unigenitus*, Only Begotten) stands on the *tetrapeza* (four-footed table). Christ is the head of the Church. As God, he is the unity of the Trinity, and as the historical Son of Man and anthropos he is the prototype of the individual inner man and at the same time the culmination, goal and totality of the empirical man. Thus we arrive at an apparently fortuitous picture of a hierosgamos taking place in the heavens, followed by the birth of a saviour and his epiphany on earth.

The picture is distinguished by a strongly marked horizontal axis. The vertical axis is expressed by the quaternity, and, more dramatically, by the heavenly origin of the fire. The comparison with a bombing is not so far-fetched, since at the time the picture was painted this possibility was in the air, both as a memory of the past and as a premonition of the future. The UFOs in the sky and the remarkable happenings down below together constitute an impressive vertical, which could be interpreted as the intrusion of a different order of things. The accent lies without doubt on the quincunx, which we have dealt with above. It is a decidedly enigmatic structure, and this obviously accords with the artist's intention. He has undoubtedly succeeded in expressing the bleakness, coldness, lifelessness, the cosmic "inhumanness" and infinite desolation of the horizontal, despite the association "city". He thus confirms the tendency of this kind of modern art to make the object unrecognizable and to cut off the sympathy and understanding of the beholder, who, rebuffed and confused, feels thrown back on himself.

The psychological effect is very like that of the Rorschach test, where a purely fortuitous and irrational picture appeals to the irrational powers of the imagination and brings the observer's unconscious into play. When his extraverted interest is snubbed in this way it falls back on the "subjective factor" and increases the latter's energy charge, a phenomenon that was observed very clearly in the original association tests. The isolated stimulus word uttered by the experimenter bewilders and embarrasses the subject because it may have more than one meaning. He does not quite know what to answer, and this accounts for the extraordinary variety of answers in these tests and—what is more important—for the large number of disturbed reactions[9] which are caused by the intrusion of unconscious contents.

The rebuffing of interest by unintelligibility results in its introversion and a constellation of the unconscious. Modern art has the same effect. We can therefore attribute to it a conscious or unconscious intention to turn the beholder's eyes away from the intelligible and enjoyable world of the senses, and to enforce a revelation of the unconscious as a kind of substitute for the loss of human surroundings. This is also the intention of the association experiment and the Rorschach test: they are meant to supply information concerning the background of consciousness, and this they do with great success. The experimental set-up of modern art is evidently the same: it faces the observer with the question "How will you react? What do you think? What kind of fantasy will come up?" In other words, modern art is less concerned with the pictures it produces than with the observer and his involuntary reactions. He peers at the colours on the canvas, his interest is aroused, but all he can discover is a product that defies human understanding. He feels disappointed, and already he is thrown back on a subjective reaction which vents itself in all sorts of exclamations. Anyone who knows how to interpret these will learn a lot about the subjective disposition of the observer but next to nothing about the painting as such. For him it is no more than a psychological test. This may sound disparaging, but only for those who regard the subjective factor merely as a source of discomfort. But if they are interested in their own psyches, they will try to submit their constellated complexes to closer scrutiny.

Since even the boldest fantasy of the creative artist—however much it may exceed the bounds of intelligibility—is always bounded by the limits of the psyche itself, there may easily

[9] Inhibitions, faults, slips of the tongue, subsequent forgetting of the answers, etc. All these are "complex-indicators".

appear in his pictures unknown forms which indicate certain limiting and predetermined factors. These, in Tanguy's picture, are the quincunx, the quaternity with the 3 + 1 structure, and the "signs in the heavens", the circles and the cigar-form—in a word, the archetypes. In its attempt to leave the world of visible and intelligible appearances and to float in the boundlessness of chaos, modern art, to a still greater degree than the psychological tests, evokes complexes which have sloughed off their usual personal aspect and appear as what they originally were, namely primordial forms of the instincts. They are of a suprapersonal, collective-unconscious nature. Personal complexes arise wherever there are conflicts with the instinctual make-up. These are the points of faulty adaptation, and their sensitiveness releases affects which tear the mask of adaptedness off the face of civilized man. This also seems to be the goal that modern art is indirectly aiming at. For all the appearance of extreme arbitrariness and boundless chaos, the loss of beauty and meaning is compensated by a strengthening of the unconscious. And since this is not chaotic but pertains to the natural order of things, it is to be expected that forms and patterns will arise which are indicative of this order. This seems to be the case in the examples we have been discussing. As though by chance there appear in the chaos of possibilities unexpected ordering principles which have the closest affinities with the timeless psychic dominants, but at the same time have conjured up a collective fantasy typical of our technological age and painted it in the skies.

Pictures of this kind are rather rare, but not undiscoverable. For that matter, relatively few people have seen an UFO, yet there can be no doubt about the existence of the rumour. It has even attracted the attention of hard-headed military authorities, despite the fact that for sheer improbability it outdoes anything I have said about the meaning of the pictures. Anyone who wants to get an independent idea of the scope of the UFO legend should read Edgar Sievers' *Flying Saucers über Sudafrika*.[10] Though open to attack at many points, it gives one some notion of the efforts an intelligent and well-meaning person has to make in order to come to terms with the UFOs. It is undoubtedly a challenging matter that has caused the author to move heaven and hell. What he unfortunately lacks is a knowledge of the psychology of the unconscious, perhaps the most important thing here. His book sets forth all the earlier and recent attempts at explanation based on scientific and philosophical premises, but also, unfortunately, on unverifiable theosophical assertions. Lack of discrimination and credulity, which elsewhere would be vices, here serve the useful purpose of bringing together a collection of hetero-geneous speculations on the UFO problem. Anyone who is inter-ested in the psychology of the rumour will read this book with profit, for it offers a comprehensive survey of the psychic phenomenology of the UFO.

[10] Sagittarius Verlag, Pretoria, 1955.

4

PREVIOUS HISTORY OF THE UFO PHENOMENON

Though the UFOs were first publicized only towards the end of the Second World War, the phenomenon itself was known long before. It was observed in the first half of this century, and was described in earlier centuries and perhaps even in antiquity. In the UFO literature there are collections of reports from various sources which need critically evaluating. I shall spare myself this task and give the reader only two examples.

FIGURE 1: BASEL BROADSHEET, 1566

This is from a broadsheet written by Samuel Coccius, "student of the Holy Scripture and of the free arts, at Basel, in the Fatherland", in August 1566. He reports that on August 7th of that year, at the time of the sunrise, "many large black globes were seen in the air, moving before the sun with great speed, and turning against each other as if fighting. Some of them became red and fiery and afterwards faded and went out."

Figure 1 Basel Broadsheet, 1566

As the illustration shows, this sighting was made in Basel. The dark colour of the UFOs may be due to their having been seen against the light of the rising sun. Some of them were bright and fiery. Their speed and irregular motion are typical UFO features.

FIGURE 2: NUREMBERG BROADSHEET, 1561

The broadsheet comes from Nuremberg and relates the story of a "very frightful spectacle" seen by "numerous men and women" at sunrise on April 14th 1561. They saw "globes" of a blood-red, bluish, or black colour, or "plates" in large numbers near the sun, "some three in a row, now and then four in a square, also some standing alone. And amongst these globes some blood-coloured crosses were seen." Moreover there were "two great tubes"—three in the picture—"in which three, four and more globes were to be seen. They all began to fight one

Figure 2 Nuremberg Broadsheet, 1561
Both Broadsheets from the Wickiana Collection, Zürich Central Library

another." This went on for about an hour. Then "they all fell—as one sees in the picture—from the sun and sky down to the earth, as if everything were on fire, then it slowly faded away on the earth, producing a lot of steam." Underneath the globes a long object was seen, "shaped like a great black spear". Naturally this "spectacle" was interpreted as a divine warning.

This report, as the reader will have noted, contains certain details already known to us. Above all the "tubes", which are analogous to the cylindrical objects in the UFO reports. These, in UFO language, are the "motherships" which are said to carry the smaller, lens-shaped UFOs for long distances. The picture shows them in operation, releasing UFOs or taking them on board. Especially important, though lacking in the modern UFO reports, are the indubitable quaternities, seen sometimes as simple crosses, sometimes as disks in the form of a cross, that is, as regular mandalas. There also seems to be a hint of the 3 + 1 motif in the dilemma of three and four. The militaristic interpretation is as characteristic of the 16th century as the technological one is of ours. The tubes are cannons and the globes cannonballs, and the shooting to and fro of the globes is an artillery engagement. The great black spearhead, as well as the spearshafts (?), seem to represent the masculine element, especially in its "penetrating" capacity. Similar things are reported in the UFO literature.

The emphasis on the cross motif is striking. The Christian meaning of the cross can hardly be considered here, since we are dealing with a natural phenomenon, a swarm of round objects in violent motion, shooting in opposite directions and reminding the reporter of a battle. If the UFOs were living organisms, one would think of a swarm of insects rising with the sun, not to fight one another but to mate and celebrate the marriage flight. Here the cross signifies a union of opposites (vertical and horizontal), a "crossing"; as a plus sign, it is also a joining together, an addition. Where the globes are coupled together to form quaternities, they have given rise to the crossed marriage quaternio, which I have discussed in my "Psychology of the Transference".[1] It forms the model for the primitive "cross cousin marriage", but is also an individuation symbol, the union of the "four".

Columns of smoke rise up from the place where the cannonballs have fallen, reminding us of Tanguy's picture. The moment of sunrise, the *Aurora consurgens* (Aquinas, Boehme), suggests the revelation of the light. Both reports have clear analogies not only with one another but also with the modern saucer stories and with the individual products of the unconscious today.

---

[1] Cf. *The Practice of Psychotherapy*, Coll. Works, vol. 16, pp. 211ff.

Figure 3 The Spiritual Pilgrim Discovering Another World

FIGURE 3: THE SPIRITUAL PILGRIM DISCOVERING ANOTHER WORLD

This 17th-century engraving, possibly representing a Rosicrucian illumination, comes from a source unknown to me.[2] On the right it shows the familiar world. The pilgrim, who is evidently on a *pélerinage de l'âme*, has broken through the star-strewn rim of his world and beholds another, supernatural universe filled with what look like layers of cloud or mountain ranges. In it appear the wheels of Ezekiel and rings or rainbow-like figures, obviously representing the "heavenly spheres". In these symbols we have a prototype of the UFO empirical vision, which is vouchsafed to the illuminati. They cannot be heavenly bodies belonging to our world, but are projected "rotunda" from the inner, four-dimensional world. This is even more evident in the next picture.

[2] It was kindly placed at my disposal by D. van Houten, Bergen. Holland.

FIGURE 4: THE QUICKENING OF THE CHILD IN THE WOMB

This picture comes from the Rupertsberg Codex "Scivias", written by Hildegard of Bingen (12th cent.). It shows the quickening or "animation" of the child in the body of the mother. From a higher world an influx enters the foetus. This upper world has a remarkable quadratic form divided into three to correspond with the Trinity, but, unlike the latter, which is supposed to consist of three equal parts, the middle section is different from the other two. It contains round objects, whereas the other two are characterized by the eye motif. Like the wheels of Ezekiel in the Bible, these little rotunda are associated with eyes.

As Hildegard's text states, the radiance of the "countless eyes" (there are in reality twenty-four in each section) means "God's knowledge", that is, his seeing and knowing, with reference to the seven eyes of God that "run to and fro through the whole earth" (Zech. 4: 10). The rotunda, on the other hand, are God's deeds, such as the sending of his son as a saviour (p. 127). Hildegard adds: "All, the bad as well as the good, appear in God's knowledge, for it is not ever clouded round by any darkness". The souls of men are "fireballs" (pp. 120, 126, 130, 133), so presumably the soul of Christ was also such a ball, for Hildegard interprets her vision not with reference to the growth of a human child only, but with particular reference to Christ and the Mother of God (p. 127). The square divided into three stands for the Holy Ghost entering into the child (p. 129). The procreative aspect of the Holy Ghost unites the Godhead with matter, as is clear from the sacred legend. The intermediate forms between spirit and matter are obviously the rotunda, early stages of animated bodies, filling the middle section of the square. There are thirty of them, and, however accidental this may be, the number thirty (days of the month) suggests the moon, ruler of the hylical world, whereas twenty-four (hours of the day) suggests the sun,

Figure 4 The Quickening of the Child in the Womb

(Reproduced by kind permission of the Otto Müller Verlag, Salzburg. From Hildegard of Bingen, *Wisse die Wege. Scivias*, trans. and ed. by Maria Böckeler, Salzburg. 1954.)

the king. This indicates the motif of the *coniunctio* ($\odot$ and $\mathbb{D}$)—an instance of that unconscious readiness which later came to expression in Cusanus' definition of God as a *complexio oppositorum*. In the miniature the rotunda are fire-coloured, the fiery seeds from which human beings will sprout, a sort of pneumatic roe. This comparison is justified in so far as alchemy compares the rotunda to fish's eyes. The eyes of a fish are always open, like the eyes of God. They are synonymous with the *scintillae*, "soul sparks". It is just possible that these alchemical allusions crept into Hildegard's text via the atoms of Democritus (*spiritus insertus atomis*).[4] Another such source may be responsible for the squareness of the Holy Ghost.

The square, being a quaternity, is a totality symbol in alchemy. Having four corners it signifies the earth, whereas a circular form is attributed to the spirit. Earth is feminine, spirit masculine. The square as a symbol of the spiritual world is certainly most unusual, but becomes more intelligible when we take Hildegard's sex into account. This remarkable symbolism is reflected in the squaring of the circle—another *coniunctio oppositorum*. "Squareness" in alchemy is an important feature of the unitary substance, the *Mercurius Philosophorum sive quadratus*, and characterizes its chthonic nature, which it possesses along with spirituality (*spiritus mercurialis*). It is as much a metal as a spirit. Correspondingly, in Christian dogma, the Holy Ghost as the third person of the Trinity does not remain a prerogative of the incarnate God, but may descend also upon sinful man. Though these ideas were not yet explicitly conscious in Hildegard's day, they were implicitly present in the collective unconscious, activated by the Christ analogy. This reached consciousness in the next century, but had been clearly anticipated in the writings of Zosimos of Panopolis in the third century A.D. We must emphasize, however, that there can hardly be any historical

[4] *Somn. Scip.*, I, 14, 19.

connection between the two; it is more a question of the activated archetype of the Primordial Man or Anthropos.

Equally characteristic of alchemy is the arithmetical structure of the Holy Ghost: he is a unity, consists of two principles (eyes and fireballs), has three parts, and is a square. This motif is known under the name of the Axiom of Maria, who lived in Alexandria in the third century and played a great role in classical alchemy.

The two human groups in the picture typify the fates that preside over the awakening of the soul. There are, as Hildegard says, "people who prepare good or middling or bad cheese".[5] The devil, too, has a hand in the game. The picture shows clearly, like the previous one, that the eyes and fireballs are not identical with the heavenly bodies and are differentiated from the stars in the background. It confirms that the fireballs are souls.

SUMMARY

From the dream examples and the pictures it is evident that the unconscious, in order to portray its contents, makes use of certain fantasy elements which can be compared with the UFO phenomenon. In dreams 1, 2, 6, and 7, and in the painting of the Fire Sower, the connection with UFOs was conscious, while in the other dreams and in two of the paintings no conscious

---

[5] "You look further and see people on the earth who carry milk in clay vessels. From this they prepare cheese. They are the people, men and women, who carry human seed in their bodies. From it arise the various generations of men. Part of the milk is fatty. It makes fatty cheese. This seed . . . produces energetic people . . . In cleverness and discretion they master life and flourish in their works visibly before God and men. The devil does not find his place in them. Other milk is thin. This curdles into insipid cheese. This seed . . . produces weakly people . . . A last part of the milk is mixed with corruption, and the cheese that comes from it is bitter. This seed . . . produces malformed people", etc. *Scivias*, pp. 128f.

connection could be proved. The personal relationship between the UFO and the observing dream subject was stressed in some of the dreams, but this is completely lacking in the paintings. In medieval paintings the personal participation in an epiphany or in suchlike visionary experiences is expressed by the visible presence of the recipient of the vision. This view does not fit at all into the programme of modern art, which is more concerned to put as great a distance as possible between the object and the spectator—like the Rorschach ink blot, which is intentionally *tachist* in order to avoid any suggestion of meaning and to produce a purely subjective phantasm.

The dreams as well as the paintings, when subjected to careful scrutiny, yield a meaningful content which could be described as an epiphany. In the Fire Sower this meaning can be recognized without difficulty. In the other cases an investigation in the light of comparative psychology leads to the same conclusion. For those unacquainted with the psychology of the unconscious I must emphasize that my conclusions are not the product of unbridled fantasy, as is often supposed, but are based on thorough researches into the history of symbols. It was merely in order to avoid overloading my text with annotations that I omitted practically all the references to source material. Anyone, therefore, who feels the need to test the correctness of my conclusions will have to go to the trouble of familiarizing himself with my other writings. The amplificatory method I have used for interpreting the meaning has proved fruitful when applied to historical as well as contemporary material. In the presence instance it seems to me sufficiently safe to conclude that in my examples a central archetype consistently appears, which I have called the archetype of the self. It takes the traditional form of an epiphany from heaven, whose nature is in several cases markedly antithetical, e.g., fire and water, corresponding to the "shield of David", ✡, which consists of $\triangle$ = fire and ∇ = water. The hexad is a totality symbol: 4 as the natural division of the circle, 2 as the vertical axis (zenith and nadir)—a spatial conception of totality. As a modern development of this symbol we would cite the fourth dimension in Plates 2 and 3.

The masculine–feminine antithesis appears in the long and round objects: cigar-form and circle. These may be sexual symbols. The Chinese symbol of the one being, Tao, consists of yang (fire, hot, dry, south side of the mountain, masculine, etc.) and yin (dark, moist, cool, north side of the mountain, feminine). It fully corresponds, therefore, to the Jewish symbol mentioned above. The Christian equivalent can be found in the Church's doctrine of the unity of mother and son and in the androgynity of Christ, not to mention the hermaphroditic Primordial Being in many oriental and primitive religions, the "Father–Mother" of the Gnostics, and the Mercurius hermaphroditus of alchemy.

The third antithesis is between Above and Below, as in Plate 3, where it seems to have been moved into the fourth dimension. In the other examples it constitutes the difference between what happens in the heavens and down below on earth.

The fourth antithesis, unity and quaternity, appears united in the quincunx (Plates 3 and 4), the four forming, as it were, a frame for the one, accentuated as the centre. In the history of symbols, quaternity is the unfolding of unity. The one universal Being cannot be known, because it is not differentiated from anything and cannot be compared with anything. By unfolding into four it acquires distinct characteristics and can therefore be known. This is not a metaphysical argument but simply a psychological formula for describing the process by which an unconscious content becomes conscious. So long as a thing is in the unconscious it has no recognizable qualities and is consequently merged with the universal unknown, with the unconscious All and Nothing, with what the Gnostics called a "non-existent all-being". But as soon as the unconscious content enters the sphere of consciousness it has already split into the "four", that is to say it can become an object of experience only by virtue of the four basic functions of consciousness. It is *perceived* as something that exists (sensation); it is *recognized* as this and *distinguished* from that (thinking); it is *evaluated* as pleasant or unpleasant, etc. (feeling); and finally, intuition tells us where it came from and where it is going. This cannot be perceived by the senses or thought by the intellect. Consequently the object's extension in time and what happens to it is the proper concern of intuition. The splitting into four has the same significance as the division of the horizon into four quarters, or of the year into four seasons. That is, through the act of becoming conscious the four basic aspects of a whole judgement are rendered visible. This naturally does nothing to stop the speculative intellect from thinking up 101 other aspects. The four we have named are nothing more than a natural, minimal division of the circle or totality. In my work with patients the quaternity symbol crops up very frequently, the pentad very rarely, and rather less rarely the triad. Since my practice was always cosmopolitan I had plenty of occasion for comparative ethnological observations, and it struck me that the triadic mandalas invariably came from Germans. This seemed to me to have some connection with the fact that, compared with French and Anglo-Saxon literature, the typical anima figure in German novels plays a relatively insignificant role. From a totality standpoint the triadic mandala has a $4 - 1$ structure as opposed to the usual $3 + 1$. The fourth function is the undifferentiated or inferior function which characterizes the shadow side of the personality. When this is missing in the totality symbol there is too much emphasis on the conscious side.

The fifth antithesis concerns the contrast between an enigmatic higher world and the ordinary human world. This is the most important polarity, which is illustrated in all the examples and can therefore be taken as fundamental both to the dreams and to the pictures. The contrast seems to be intentional as well as being very striking, and, if we take this feeling into account, appears to convey something like a message. The horizontal axis of our empirical consciousness, which except for psychic contents is aware only of bodies in motion, is crossed by another order of being, a dimension of the "psychic"—for the only statements we can safely make about this other order refer to the psychic, something on the one hand *mathematically abstract* and on the other hand *fabulous and mythological*. Now if we conceive numbers as having been *discovered*, and not merely *invented* as an instrument for counting, then on account of their mythological nature they belong to the realm of "godlike" human and animal figures and are just as archetypal as they. Unlike these, however, they are "real" in the sense that they are encountered in the realm of experience as quantities and thus form the bridge between the tangible, physical world and the imaginary. Though the latter is unreal, it is "real" in so far as it works, i.e., has an effect on us. There can be no doubt about its effectiveness, particularly at the present time. It is not the behaviour, the lack or surplus, of physical things that directly affects humanity so much as the idea we have of them, or the "imaginary" ideas by which we are obsessed.

The role that numbers play in mythology and in the unconscious gives food for thought. They are an aspect of the physically real as well as of the psychically imaginary. They do not only count and measure, and are not merely quantitative; they also make qualitative statements and are therefore a mysterious something midway between myth and reality, partly discovered and partly invented. Equations, for instance, which were invented as pure mathematical formulae, have subsequently proved to be formulations of the quantitative behaviour of physical things. Conversely, owing to their individual qualities, numbers can be vehicles for psychic processes in the unconscious. The structure of the mandala, for instance, is intrinsically mathematical. We may exclaim with the mathematician Jacobi: "In the Olympian host Number eternally reigns".

These hints are merely intended to point out to the reader that the opposition between the human world and the higher world is not absolute; the two are only relatively incommensurable, for the bridge between them is not entirely lacking. Between them stands the great mediator, Number, whose reality is valid in both worlds, as an archetype in its very essence. Deviation into theosophical speculation does not help us to understand the splitting of the world picture indicated in our examples, for this is simply a matter of names and words which do not point the way to the *unus mundus* (unitary world). Number, however, belongs to both worlds, the real and the imaginary; it is visible and invisible, quantitative and qualitative.

Thus it is a fact of singular importance that number also characterizes the "personal" nature of the mediating figure, that is appears as a mediator. From the psychological standpoint, and having regard to the limits set to all scientific knowledge, I have called the mediating or "uniting" symbol which necessarily proceeds from a sufficiently great tension of opposites the "self". I chose this term in order to make clear that I am concerned primarily with the formulation of empirical facts and not with dubious incursions into metaphysics. There I would trespass upon all manner of religious convictions. Living in the West, I would have to say Christ instead of "self", in the Near East it would be Khidr, in the Far East atman or Tao or the Buddha, in the Far West maybe a hare or Mondamin, and in cabalism it would be Tifereth. Our world has shrunk, and it is dawning on us that humanity is *one*, with *one* psyche, that humility is a not inconsiderable virtue which should prompt Christians, for the sake of charity—the greatest of all virtues—to set a good example and acknowledge that though there is only *one* truth it speaks in many tongues, and that if we still cannot see this it is simply due to lack of understanding. No one is so godlike that he alone knows the true word. All of us gaze into that "dark glass" in which the dark myth takes shape, adumbrating the invisible truth. In this glass the eyes of the spirit glimpse an image which we call the self, fully conscious of the fact that it is an anthropomorphic image which we have merely named but not explained. By "self" we mean psychic wholeness, but what realities underlie this concept we do not know, because psychic contents cannot be observed in their unconscious state, and moreover the psyche cannot know itself. The conscious can know the unconscious only so far as it has become conscious. We have only a very hazy idea of the changes an unconscious content undergoes in the process of becoming conscious, but no certain knowledge. The concept of psychic wholeness necessarily implies an element of transcendence on account of the existence of unconscious components. Transcendence in this sense is not equivalent to a metaphysical postulate or hypostasis; it claims to be no more than a borderline concept, to quote Kant.

That there is something beyond the borderline, beyond the frontiers of knowledge, is shown by the archetypes and, most clearly of all, by numbers, which this side of the border are quantities but on the other side are autonomous psychic entities, capable of making qualitative statements which manifest themselves in *a priori* patterns of order. These patterns include not only causally explicable phenomena like dream symbols and such, but remarkable relativizations of time and space which simply cannot be explained causally. These are the parapsychological phenomena which I have summed up under the term "synchronicity" and which have been statistically investigated by Rhine. The positive results of his experiments elevate these phenomena to the rank of undeniable facts. This brings us a little nearer to understanding the mystery of psychophysical parallelism, for we now know that a factor exists which mediates between the apparent incommensurability of body and psyche, giving matter a kind of "psychic" faculty and the psyche a kind of "materiality", by means of which the one can work on the other. That the body can work on the psyche seems to be a truism, but strictly speaking all we know is that any bodily defect or illness also expresses itself psychically. Naturally this assumption only holds good if, contrary to the popular materialistic view, the psyche is credited with an existence of its own. But materialism in its turn cannot explain how chemical changes can produce a psyche. Both views, the materialistic as well as the spiritualistic, are metaphysical prejudices. It accords better with experience to suppose that living matter has a psychic aspect, and the psyche a physical aspect. But if we give due consideration to the facts of parapsychology, then the hypothesis of the psychic aspect must be extended beyond the sphere of biochemical processes to matter in general. In that case all reality would be grounded on an as-yet-unknown substrate possessing material and at the same time psychic qualities. In view of the trend of modern theoretical physics, this assumption should arouse fewer resistances than before. It would also do away with the awkward hypothesis of psychophysical parallelism, and afford us an opportunity to construct a new world model closer to the idea of the *unus mundus*. The "acausal" correspondences between mutually independent psychic and physical events, i.e., synchronistic phenomena, and in particular psychokinesis, would then become more understandable, for every physical event would involve a psychic one and vice versa. Such reflections are not idle speculations; they are forced on us in any serious psychological investigation of the UFO phenomenon, as the next chapter will show.

5

UFOS CONSIDERED IN A NON-PSYCHOLOGICAL LIGHT

As I said at the beginning, it was the purpose of this essay to treat the UFOs primarily as a psychological phenomenon. There were plenty of reasons for this, as is abundantly clear from the contradictory and "impossible" assertions made by the rumour. It is quite right that they should meet with criticism, scepticism, and open rejection, and if anyone should see behind them nothing more than a phantasm that deranges the minds of men and engenders rationalistic resistances, he would have nothing but our sympathy. Indeed, since conscious and unconscious fantasy, and even mendacity, obviously play an important role in building up the rumour, we could be satisfied with the psychological explanation and let it rest at that.

Unfortunately, however, there are good reasons why the UFOs cannot be disposed of in this simple manner. So far as I know it remains an established fact, supported by numerous observations, that UFOs have not only been seen visually but have also been picked up on the radar screen and have left traces on the photographic plate. I base myself here not only on the comprehensive reports by Ruppelt and Keyhoe, which leave no room for doubt in this regard, but also on the fact that the astrophysicist, Professor Menzel, has not succeeded, despite all his efforts, in offering a satisfying scientific explanation of even one authentic UFO report. It boils down to nothing less than this: that either psychic projections throw back a radar echo, or else the appearance of real objects affords an opportunity for mythological projections.

Here I must remark that even if the UFOs are physically real, the corresponding psychic projections are not actually caused, but are only occasioned, by them. Mythical statements of this kind have always occurred, whether UFOs exist or not. These statements depend in the first place on the peculiar nature of the psychic background, the collective unconscious, and for this reason have always been projected in some form. At various times all sorts of other projections have appeared in the heavens besides the saucers. This particular projection, together with its psychological context, the rumour, is specific of our age and highly characteristic of it. The dominating idea of a mediator and god who became man, after having thrust the old polytheistic beliefs into the background, is now in its turn on the point of evaporating. Untold millions of so-called Christians have lost their belief in a real and living mediator, while the believers endeavour to make their belief credible to primitive people, when it would be so much more fruitful to bestow these much needed efforts on the white man. But it is always so much easier and more affecting to talk and act down to people instead of up to them. St Paul spoke to the populace of Athens and Rome, but what is Albert Schweitzer doing in Lambarene? People like him are needed much more urgently in Europe.

No Christian will contest the importance of a belief like that of the mediator, nor will he deny the consequences which the loss of it entails. So powerful an idea reflects a profound psychic need which does not simply disappear when the expression of it ceases to be valid. What happens to the energy that once kept the idea alive and dominant over the psyche? A political, social, philosophical, and religious conflict of unprecedented proportions has split the consciousness of our age. When such tremendous opposites split asunder, we may expect with certainty that the need for a saviour will make itself felt. Experience has amply confirmed that, in the psyche as in nature, a tension of opposites creates a potential which may express itself at any time in a manifestation of energy. Between above and below flows the waterfall, and between hot and cold there is a turbulent exchange of molecules. Similarly, between the psychic opposites there is generated a "uniting symbol", at first unconscious. This process is running its course in the unconscious of modern man. Between the opposites there arises spontaneously a symbol of unity and wholeness, no matter whether it reaches consciousness or not. Should something extraordinary or impressive then occur in the outside world, be it a human personality, a thing, or an idea, the unconscious content can project itself upon it, thereby investing the projection carrier with numinous and mythical powers. Thanks to its numinosity, the projection carrier has a highly suggestive effect and grows into a saviour myth whose basic features have been repeated countless times.

The impetus for the manifestation of the latent psychic contents was given by the UFO. The only thing we know with tolerable certainty about UFOs is that they possess a surface which can be seen by the eye and at the same time throws back a radar echo. Everything else is so uncertain that it must remain for the time being an unproven conjecture, or rumour, until we know more about it. We do not know, either, whether they are manned machines or a species of living creature which has appeared in our atmosphere from an unknown source. It is not likely that they are meteoric phenomena, since their behaviour does not give the impression of a process that could be interpreted in physical terms. Their movements indicate volition and psychic relatedness, e.g., evasion and flight, perhaps even aggression and defence. Their progression in space is not in a straight line and of constant velocity like a meteor, but erratic like the flight of an insect and of varying velocity, from zero to several thousand miles per hour. The observed speeds and angles of turn are such that no earthly being could survive them any more than he could the enormous heat generated by friction.

The simultaneous visual and radar sightings would in themselves be a satisfactory proof of their reality. Unfortunately, well-authenticated reports show that there are also cases where the eye sees something that does not appear on the radar screen, or where an object undoubtedly picked up by radar is not seen by the eye. I will not mention other, even more remarkable reports from authoritative sources; they are so bizarre that they tax our understanding and credulity to the limit.

If these things are real—and by all human standards it hardly seems possible to doubt this any longer—then we are left with only two hypotheses: that of their *weightlessness* on the one hand and of their *psychic nature* on the other. This is a question I for one cannot decide. In the circumstances, however, it seemed to me advisable at least to investigate the *psychological aspect* of the phenomenon, so as to throw a little light on this complicated situation. I have limited myself to only a few examples. Unfortunately, after more than ten years' study of the problem I have not managed to collect a sufficient number of observations from which more reliable conclusions could be drawn. I must therefore content myself with having sketched out a few lines for future research. Of course, next to nothing has been gained as regards the physical explanation of the phenomenon. But the psychic aspect plays so great a role that it cannot be left out of account. The discussion of it, as I have tried to show, leads to psychological problems which involve just as fantastic possibilities or impossibilities as the approach from the physical side.

If military authorities have felt compelled to set up bureaus for collecting and evaluating UFO reports, then psychology, too, has not only the right but also the duty to do what it can to shed light on this dark problem.

The question of anti-gravity is one which I must leave to the physicists, who alone can inform us what chances of success such an hypothesis has. The alternative hypothesis that UFOs are something psychic that is equipped with certain physical properties seems even less probable, for where should such a thing come from? If weightlessness is a hard hypothesis to swallow, then the notion of a materialized psychism opens a bottomless void under our feet. Parapsychology is, of course, acquainted with the fact of materialization. But this phenomenon depends on the presence of one or more mediums who exude a weighable substance, and it occurs only in their immediate environment. The psyche can move the body, but only inside the living organism. That something psychic, possessing material qualities and with a high charge of energy, could appear by itself high in the air at a great distance from any human mediums—this surpasses our comprehension. Here our knowledge leaves us completely in the lurch, and it is therefore pointless to speculate any further in this direction.

It seems to me—speaking with all due reserve—that there is a third possibility: that UFOs are real material phenomena of an unknown nature, presumably coming from outer space, which perhaps have long been visible to mankind, but otherwise have no recognizable connection with the earth or its inhabitants. In recent times, however, and just at the moment when the eyes of mankind are turned towards the heavens, partly on account of their fantasies about possible spaceships, and partly in a figurative sense because their earthly existence feels threatened, unconscious contents have projected themselves on these inexplicable heavenly phenomena and given them a significance they in no way deserve. Since they seem to have appeared more frequently after the Second World War than before, it may be that they are synchronistic phenomena or "meaningful co-incidences". The psychic situation of mankind and the UFO phenomenon as a physical reality bear no recognizable causal relationship to one another, but they seem to coincide in a meaningful manner. The meaningful connection is the product on the one hand of the projection and on the other of the round and cylindrical forms which embody the projected meaning and have always symbolized the union of opposites.

Another equally "chance" coincidence is the choice of the national emblems for aircraft in the USSR and the USA: respect-ively a red and white five-pointed star. For a thousand years red was regarded as the masculine and white as the feminine colour. The alchemists spoke of the *servus rubeus* (red slave) and the *femina candida* (white woman): their copulation produced the supreme union of opposites. When one speaks of Russia, one immedi-ately thinks of "Little Father" Czar and "Little Father" Stalin. One also remembers all the talk about America being a matriarchy because the bulk of American capital is in the hands of women, not to mention Keyserling's *bon mot* about the "aunt of the nation". It is clear that these parallels have nothing to do with the choice of symbols, at any rate not as a conscious causality. Com-ically enough—one must say—red and white are the nuptial colours. They throw an amusing light on Soviet Russia as the reluctant or unrequited lover of the *femina candida* in the White House—even if there is nothing more to it than that.

EPILOGUE

I had already completed my manuscript when a little book fell into my hands, which I ought not to leave unmentioned: *The Secret of the Saucers*, by Orfeo M. Angelucci (Amherst Press, 1955). The author is self-taught and describes himself as a nervous individual suffering from "constitutional inadequacy". After working at various jobs he was employed as a mechanic in 1952 at the Lockheed Aircraft Corporation at Burbank, California. He seems to lack any kind of mental culture, but appears to have a knowledge of science that exceeds what would be expected of a person in his circumstances. He is an Americanized Italian, naïve and—if appearances do not deceive us—serious and idealistic. He makes his living now by preaching the gospel revealed to him by the saucers. That is the reason why I mention his book.

His career as a prophet began with the sighting of a sup- posedly authentic UFO on August 4th, 1946. At the time he had no further interest in the problem. He was working in his free hours on a book entitled "The Nature of Infinite Entities", which he subsequently published at his own expense. He describes its content as "Atomic Evolution, Suspension, and Involution, Origin of the Cosmic Rays", etc. On May 23rd 1952, he underwent the experience that gave him his calling. Towards 11 o'clock in the evening, he says, he felt unwell and had a "prickling" sensation in the upper half of his body, as before an electrical storm. He was working nightshift, and as he was driving home in his car he saw a faintly red-glowing, oval-shaped object hovering over the horizon, which nobody else seemed to see. On a lonely stretch of the road, where it rose above the level of the surrounding terrain, he saw below him the glowing red disk "pulsating" near the ground only a short distance away. Suddenly it shot upwards with great speed at an angle of 30–40 degrees and disappeared towards the west. But before it vanished, it released two balls of green fire from which a man's voice issued, speaking "perfect English". He could remember the words: "Don't be afraid, Orfeo, we are friends!" The voice bade him get out of the car. This he did, and, leaning against the car, he watched the two "pulsating" disks hovering a short distance in front of him. The voice explained to him that the lights were "instruments of transmission and reception" (i.e., a species of sense organs) and that he was in direct communication with "friends from another world". It also asked him if he remembered his experience on August 4th, 1946. All at once he felt very thirsty, and the voice told him: "Drink from the crystal cup you will find on the fender of your car". He drank, and it was the "most delicious beverage I had ever tasted". He felt refreshed and strengthened. The twin disks were about three feet apart. "Suddenly the area between them began to glow with a soft green light which gradually formed into a luminous three-dimensional screen." In it there appeared the heads and shoulders of two persons, a man and a woman, "being the ultimate of perfection". They had large shining eyes, and despite their supernatural perfection they seemed strangely familiar to him. They observed him and the whole scene. It seemed to him that he was in telepathic communication with them. As suddenly as it had come the vision vanished, and the fireballs reassumed their former brilliance. He heard the words: "The road will open, Orfeo", and the voice continued:

> We see the individuals of Earth as each one really is, Orfeo, and not as perceived by the limited senses of man. The people of your planet have been under observation for centuries, but have only recently been re-surveyed. Every point of progress in your society is registered with us. We know you as you do not know yourselves. Every man, woman and child is recorded in vital statistics by means of our recording crystal disks. Each of you is infinitely more important to us than to your fellow Earthlings because you are not aware of the true mystery of your being . . . We feel a deep sense of brotherhood toward Earth's inhabitants because of an ancient kinship of our planet with Earth. In you we can look far back in time and recreate certain aspects of our former world. With deep compassion and understanding we have watched your world going through its "growing pains". We ask that you look upon us simply as older brothers.

The author was also informed that the UFOs were remote-controlled by a mothership. The occupants of UFOs needed in reality no such vessels. As "etheric" entities they needed them only in order to manifest themselves materially to man. The UFOs could travel approximately with the speed of light. "The Speed of Light is the Speed of Truth" (i.e., quick as thought). The heavenly visitors were harmless and filled with the best intentions. "Cosmic law" forbade spectacular landings on earth. The earth was at present threatened by greater dangers than was realized.

After these revelations Angelucci felt exalted and strengthened. It was "as though momentarily I had transcended mortality and was somehow related to these superior beings". When the lights disappeared, it seemed to him that the everyday world had lost its reality and become an abode of shadows.

On July 23rd 1952, he felt unwell and stayed away from work. In the evening he took a walk, and on the way back, in a lonely place, similar sensations came over him as he had felt on May 23rd. Combined with them was "the dulling of consciousness I had noted on that other occasion", i.e., the awareness of an *abaissement du niveau mental*, a state which is a very important precondition for the occurrence of spontaneous psychic phenomena. Suddenly he saw a luminous object on the ground before him, like an "igloo" or a "huge, misty soap bubble". This object visibly increased in solidity, and he saw something like a doorway leading into a brightly lit interior. He stepped inside, and found himself in a vaulted room, about eighteen feet in diameter. The walls were made of some "ethereal mother-of-pearl stuff".

Facing him was a comfortable reclining chair consisting of the same translucent, shimmering substance. Otherwise the room was empty and silent. He sat down and had the feeling that he was suspended in air. It was as if the chair moulded itself to the shape of his body of its own accord. The door shut as if there had never been a door there at all. Then he heard a kind of humming, a rhythmical sound like a vibration, which put him into a kind of semi-dream state. The room grew dark, and music came from the walls. Then it grew light again. He found on the floor a piece of metal like a coin. When he took it in his hand, it seemed to diminish in size. He had the feeling that the UFO was carrying him away. Suddenly something like a round window opened, about nine feet in diameter. Outside he saw a planet, the earth, from a distance of over a thousand miles, as a voice he recognized explained to him. He wept with emotion and the voice said: "Weep, Orfeo . . . we weep with you for earth and her children. For all its apparent beauty earth is a purgatorial world among the planets evolving intelligent life. Hate, selfishness and cruelty rise from many parts of it like a dark mist." Then, he says, the craft evidently moved out into cosmic space. Through the window he saw a UFO about 1000 feet long and 90 feet thick, consisting of a transparent, crystalline substance. Music poured from it, bringing visions of harmoniously revolving planets and galaxies. The voice informed him that every being on earth was divinely created, and "upon your world the mortal shadows of those entities are working out their salvation from the plane of darkness." All these entities were either on the good side or on the bad. "We know where you stand, Orfeo." Owing to his physical weakness he had spiritual gifts, and that was why the heavenly beings could enter into communication with him. He was given to understand that the music as well as the voice emanated from this huge spaceship. It moved off slowly, and he noticed at either end of it "vortices of flame" that served as propellers, but they were also instruments for seeing and hearing, "through some method of telepathic contact".

On the way back they met two ordinary UFOs travelling earthwards. The voice entertained him with more explanations concerning the attitude of the higher beings to mankind: man had not kept pace morally and psychologically with his techno-logical development, and therefore the inhabitants of other planets were trying to instill into the earth dwellers a better understanding of their present predicament and to help them particularly in the art of healing. They also wanted to put Orfeo right about Jesus Christ. Jesus, so they said, was called allegoric-ally the son of God. In reality he was the "Lord of the Flame", "an infinite entity of the Sun" and not of earthly origin. "As the Sun spirit who sacrificed Himself for the children of woe he has become a part of the oversoul of mankind and the world spirit. In this he differs from all other cosmic teachers."

Everyone on earth has a "spiritual, unknown self which tran-scends the material world and consciousness and dwells eter-nally outside of the Time dimension in spiritual perfection within the unity of the oversoul." The sole purpose of human existence on earth is to attain reunion with the "immortal consciousness". Under the searching eye of this "great com-passionate consciousness" Orfeo felt like a "crawling worm—unclean, filled with error and sin". He wept, once more to the accompaniment of appropriate music. The voice spoke and said: "Beloved friend of Earth, we baptize you now in the true light of the worlds eternal." A white flash of lightning blazed forth: his life lay clear before his eyes, and the remembrance of all his previous existences came back to him. He understood "the mystery of life". He thought he was going to die, for he knew that at this moment he was wafted into "eternity, into a timeless sea of bliss".

After this illuminative experience he came to himself again. Accompanied by the obligatory "etheric" music he was borne back to earth. As he left the UFO, it suddenly vanished without trace. Afterwards, on going to bed, he noticed a burning sensa-tion on the left side of his chest. There he found a stigma the size of a 25 cent bit, an inflamed circle with a dot in the middle. He interpreted this as the "symbol of the hydrogen atom".

His career as a gospeller dates—true to form—from this experience. He became a witness not only of the word but of the UFO, and was exposed to the mockery and disbelief that are the lot of the martyr. On the night of August 2nd of the same year he saw, with eight other witnesses, an ordinary UFO in the sky, which disappeared after a short time. He betook himself to the lonely spot he had previously visited, but though he didn't find the UFO he met a figure who called out to him: "Greetings, Orfeo!" It was the same figure he had seen in the earlier vision, who wished to be called by the name of "Neptune". He was a tall handsome man with unusually large and expressive eyes. The edges of the figure rippled like water in the wind. Neptune gave him more information concerning the earth, the reasons for its lamentable conditions, and its coming redemption. Then he vanished.

At the beginning of September 1953 he fell into a somnambulistic state which lasted about a week. When he returned to his normal consciousness he remembered everything he had experienced during his "absence". He had been on a small "planetoid" where Neptune dwelt with his companion Lyra; or rather, he had been in heaven as Orfeo imagined it, with count-less flowers, delightful odours, colours, nectar and ambrosia, noble etheric beings and, of course, almost incessant music. There he discovered that his heavenly friend was not called Neptune but Orion, and that "Neptune" had been his own name while he was still dwelling in this heavenly world. Lyra showed him particular marks of attention, to which he, the re-remembered Neptune, in accordance with his earthly nature, responded with erotic feelings, much to the horror of the celes-tial company. When he had dehabituated himself, with some effort, from this all-too-human reaction a *noce céleste* was cele-brated, a mystic union analogous to the *coniunctio oppositorum* in alchemy.

With this climax I will end the account of this *pélerinage de l'âme*. Without having the faintest inkling of psychology, Angelucci has described in the greatest detail the mystic experience associ-ated with a UFO vision. A detailed commentary by me is hardly necessary. The story is so naïve and clear that a reader interested in psychology can see at once how far it confirms my previous conclusions. It could even be regarded as a unique document that sheds a great deal of light on the genesis and assimilation of UFO mythology. That is why I have let Angelucci have his say.

The psychological experience that is associated with the UFO consists in the vision of the *rotundum*, the symbol of whole-ness and the archetype that expresses itself in mandala form. Mandalas, as we know, usually appear in situations of psychic confusion and perplexity. The archetype thereby constellated represents a pattern of order which, like a psychological "view-finder" marked with a cross or circle divided into four, is superimposed on the psychic chaos so that each content falls into place and the weltering confusion is held together by the protective circle. The Eastern mandalas in Mahayana Buddhism accordingly represent the cosmic, temporal, and psychological order. At the same time they are *yantras*, instruments with whose help the order is brought into being.[1]

As our time is characterized by fragmentation, confusion, and perplexity, this fact is also expressed in the psychology of the individual, appearing in spontaneous fantasy images, dreams, and the products of active imagination. I have observed these phenomena in my patients for forty years and have come to the conclusion that this archetype is of central importance, or rather, that it gains in importance to the degree that the importance of the ego is lost. A state of disorientation is particularly apt to depotentiate the ego.

Psychologically, the rotundum or mandala is a symbol of the self. The self is the archetype of order par excellence. The structure of the mandala is arithmetical, for "whole" numbers are likewise archetypes of order. This is true particularly of the number 4, the Pythagorean tetraktys. Since a state of confusion is generally the result of a psychic conflict, we find in practice that the dyad, the conjoined two, is also associated with the mandala. This appears in Angelucci's vision of the synthesis of opposites.

Its central position gives the symbol a high feeling-value, expressed for instance in Angelucci's stigmatization. The symbols of the self coincide with the God-images, as, for instance, the *complexio oppositorum* of Cusanus with the dyad, or the definition of God as a "circle whose centre is everywhere and the circumference nowhere" with Angelucci's sign of the hydrogen atom. He was marked not by the Christian stigmata but by the

---

[1] For the physiological foundations see K. W. Bash, H. Ahlenstiel and R. Kaufmann, "Ueber Präyantraformen und ein lineares Yantra", *Studien zur Analytischen Psychologie C. G. Jungs*, Zürich, 1955.

symbol of the self, of absolute wholeness or, in religious language, God. These psychological connections gave rise to the alchemical equation between Christ and the *lapis Philosophorum*.

The centre is frequently symbolized by an eye: the ever-open eye of the fish in alchemy, or the unsleeping "God's eye" of conscience, or the all-seeing sun. The same symbols are experienced today, not as external light-phenomena but as a psychic revelation. I would like to mention as an example the case of a woman who wrote down her experience in verse form (it had no connection with UFOs):

VISION

Light strikes the pebbled bottom
Of a deep blue pool.
Through swaying grass
A jewel flickers, gleams and turns,
Demands attention as I pass,
A staring fish-eye's glance
Attracts my mind and heart—
The fish, invisible as glass.

A shimmering silver moon,
The fish, assuming shape and form,
Evolves a whirling, swirling dance,
Intensity of light increasing,
The disk becomes a blazing golden sun,
Compelling deeper contemplation.

The water is the depths of the unconscious into which a ray from the light of consciousness has penetrated. A dancing disk, a fish's eye, swims down below in the inner darkness (instead of flying in the heavens), and from it arises a world-illuminating sun, an Ichthys, a *sol invictus*, an ever-open eye which reflects the eye of the beholder and is at the same time something independent of her, a rotundum that expresses the wholeness of the self and cannot be distinguished, except conceptually, from the deity. "Fish" (Ichthys) and "sun" (*novus sol*) are allegories of Christ, which like the "eye" stand for God. In the moon and sun appear the divine mother and her son-lover, as can still be seen today in many churches.

The UFO vision follows the old rule and appears in the sky. Orfeo's fantasies are played out in an obviously heavenly place and his cosmic friends bear the names of stars. If they are not antique gods and heroes they are at least angels. The author certainly lives up to his name, for just as his wife, *née* Borgianini, is in his opinion a descendant of the Borgias of unhappy memory, so he, an earthly copy of the "angels" and a messenger bringing Eleusinian tidings of immortality, must style himself a new Orpheus, divinely appointed to initiate us into the mystery of the UFO. Not even the Orphean strains are lacking. If the name is a deliberately chosen pseudonym, we can only say *è ben trovato*. But if it appears in his birth certificate, then the matter becomes more problematical. Today we can no longer suppose that a magical compulsion attaches to a mere name, else we should have to attribute a correspondingly sinister significance to his spouse, or the anima. Much as we would like to credit him with an intellectually rather limited, naïve good faith, we would have reason to suspect that a "fine Italian hand" is at work. What appears impossible from the conscious standpoint can often be arranged by the unconscious with all the craftiness of nature: *Ce que diable ne peut, femme le fait.* Be that as it may, Orfeo's book is an essentially naïve production which for that very reason reveals all the more clearly the unconscious background of the UFO phenomenon and therefore comes like a gift to the psychologist. The individuation process, the central problem of modern psychology, is plainly depicted in it in an unconscious, symbolical form which bears out our previous reflections, although the author with his somewhat primitive mentality has taken it quite literally as a concrete happening.

This epilogue was already in the press when I received word of Fred Hoyle's book, *The Black Cloud* (London, 1957). The author is a well-known authority on astro-physics, and I was already acquainted with his two impressive volumes, *The Nature of the Universe* and *Frontiers of Astronomy*. They are brilliant expositions of the latest developments in astronomy and show their author as a bold and imaginative thinker. The fact that such an author should resort to a science-fiction story aroused my curiosity, and I read the book at once. Hoyle himself, in his preface, describes it as a "frolic", a jest, and warns against anyone identifying the views of his hero, a mathematician of genius, with his own. No intelligent reader will fall into this error, of course. Nevertheless, he will hold Professor Hoyle responsible for the authorship of his book, and he will ask what it was that induced him to tackle the UFO problem.

In his "yarn" Hoyle describes how a young astronomer at the Mount Palomar observatory, while looking for supernovae to the south of Orion, discovers a dark circular patch in a dense field of stars. It is a so-called globulus, a dark cloud of gas, which, it transpires, is moving towards our solar system. At the same time, in England, considerable disturbances are detected in the orbits of Jupiter and Saturn. The reason for this is calculated by a Cambridge mathematician, the hero of our story, as a definite mass which, it then turns out, is located exactly at the spot where the Americans discovered the black cloud. This globulus, whose diameter is approximately equal to the distance of the sun from the earth, consists of hydrogen of fairly high density and is moving straight towards the earth at forty miles a second. It will reach the earth in about eighteen months. As the black cloud gets nearer, it causes first of all a terrible heat that kills off a large part of the life on earth. This is followed by a total extinction of light and a more than Egyptian darkness lasting for about a month—a *nigredo* like that described in the *Aurora Consurgens*, a treatise ascribed to St. Thomas Aquinas: "Beholding from afar I saw a great cloud looming black over all the earth, that had absorbed the [black] earth which covered my soul."[2]

When the light reappears again, there follows a period of terrible cold, which causes another appalling catastrophe. Meanwhile, the scientists in question have been shut up by the British government in their experimental location, where, thanks to the security measures they have taken, they survive the catastrophes. By observing certain remarkable ionization phenomena in the atmosphere they come to the conclusion that these are intentionally induced, and that in consequence there must be an intelligent agent in the black cloud. By means of radio they succeed in entering into communication with it, and receive answers. They learn that the cloud is five hundred million years old and is at present engaged in regenerating itself. It has taken up its position near the sun in order to recharge itself with energy. In fact, it is feeding on the sun. The scientists discover that the cloud must eliminate all radioactive substances, as these are harmful to it. This fact is also discovered by the American observers, and at their instigation the cloud is fired at with H-bombs, with the intention of "killing" it. The cloud, meanwhile, has settled in a disk round the sun, consequently threatening the earth with six-monthly eclipses of several weeks' duration. The English naturally have a host of questions to ask the cloud, including the "metaphysical" question concerning a greater Being of still greater age, and even deeper wisdom and scientific knowledge. The cloud replies that it has already discussed the matter with other globuli but is as much in the dark about it as human beings. It is willing, however, to communicate its own

[2] Cf. *Mysterium coniunctionis*, vol. 3, Zürich 1957, p. 48.

greater knowledge directly to mankind. A young physicist declares himself ready to submit to the experiment. He gets into a hypnotic condition, but dies of a sort of inflammation of the brain before being able to make any communication. The Cambridge mathematician of genius now offers himself for experiment, on the condition, accepted by the cloud, that the process of communication shall take place very much more slowly. In spite of that he falls into a delirium which ends in his death. The cloud, however, has decided to quit the solar system and seek out another region of fixed stars. The sun emerges again from obscurity and everything is as before, except for the tremendous destruction of earthly life.

It is not difficult to see that the author has here taken up the UFO problem so characteristic of our epoch: from outer space a round object approaches the earth and causes a world-wide catastrophe. Although the legend usually considers the cata-strophic political situation, or rather nuclear fission, to be the indirect cause of the UFO phenomenon, there are not a few people who suspect that the real danger lies in the appearance of UFOs themselves—namely an invasion of the earth by star-dwellers, which might give an unexpected and probably undesirable turn to our already questionable situation. The strange idea that the black cloud possesses a sort of nervous system, and a psyche or intelligence to match, is not an original invention of the author's, since speculative ufologists have already arrived at the hypothesis of a "sentient electrical field", and also at the idea that the UFOs are provisioning themselves with something on earth—water, oxygen, small organisms, etc., just as the cloud charged itself with solar energy.

The cloud causes opposite extremes of temperature and an absolute *nigredo* such as the old alchemists dreamed of. This illus-trates a characteristic aspect of the psychological problem that arises when the light of day—consciousness—is directly con-fronted with night, the collective unconscious. Opposites of

extreme intensity collide with one another, causing a disorientation and darkening of consciousness which can assume threatening proportions, as in the initial stage of a psychosis. This aspect,
i.e., the analogy with a psychic catastrophe, is shown by Hoyle in
the confrontation between the psychic content of the cloud and
the consciousness of the two unfortunate victims. Just as earthly
life is largely wiped out by the collision with the cloud, so the
psyche and the life of the two scientists are destroyed by the
collision with the unconscious. For although the "rotundum" is
a totality symbol, it usually encounters a consciousness that is
not prepared for it and does not understand it, indeed is bound
to misunderstand it and therefore cannot tolerate it, because it
perceives the totality only in projected form, outside itself, and
cannot integrate it as a subjective phenomenon. Consciousness
commits the same grave mistake as the insane person: it understands the event as a concrete external happening and not as a
subjective symbolical process. The result is that the external
world gets into hopeless disorder and is actually "destroyed", so
far as the patient loses his relationship to it. The author suggests
the analogy with psychosis by the delirious state of the victims.
It is not only the insane person who makes this fundamental
mistake, but all those who take philosophical or theosophical
speculations for objective realities and consider the mere fact
that they believe in angels as a guarantee that such things exist in
reality.

It is significant that it is the actual hero of the story, the
mathematician of genius, who meets with disaster. No author
can avoid equipping his hero with some of his own qualities and
thus betraying that at least a part of himself is invested in him.
What happens to the hero also happens symbolically to the
author. In this case it is naturally unpleasant, for it amounts to
nothing less than the fear that a collision with the unconscious
would involve the destruction of the most differentiated function. It is a widespread, in fact a normal, prejudice that deeper

insight into unconscious motives must necessarily entail a fatal disturbance of the conscious performance. The most that can happen is an alteration of the conscious attitude. Since, in our story, everything is projected outside, mankind and all organic life on earth suffer an immense loss. The author makes no particular to-do about this; it is mentioned only as a sort of by-product. From this we may infer a predominantly intellectual attitude of consciousness.

Presumably not altogether unimpressed by a hundred or more H-bombs, which might well upset its nervous system with their radioactivity, the black cloud withdraws as suddenly as it came. Nothing whatever has been learned of its contents, except that it knows as little about a metaphysical Supreme Being as we do. Nevertheless its intelligence proves unendurably high for human beings, so that it comes suspiciously near to having a divine or angel-like nature. Here the great astronomer joins hands with the naïve Angelucci.

Understood psychologically, the story describes fantasy contents whose symbolical nature demonstrates their origin in the unconscious. Whenever a confrontation of this kind occurs, there is usually an attempt at integration. This is expressed in the intention of the cloud to remain for some time near the sun, in order to feed on its energy. Psychologically this would mean that the unconscious draws strength and life from its union with the sun. The sun loses no energy, but the earth and its life, signifying man, lose a great deal. Man has to pay the costs of this invasion or irruption of the unconscious: his psychic life is threatened with the gravest injury. What, then—psychologically speaking—is the meaning of this cosmic, or rather psychic, collision? Obviously the unconscious darkens the conscious, since no rapprochement, no dialectical process takes place between their contents. For the individual this means that the cloud deprives him of solar energy, in other words his consciousness is overpowered by the unconscious. This is equivalent to a general catastrophe, such as we have experienced in National Socialism and are still experiencing in the Communist inundation, where an archaic social order threatens our freedom with tyranny and slavery. Man replies to this catastrophe with his "best" weapon. Whether for this reason or from a change of mind (as seems more likely), the cloud withdraws to other regions. This means, psychologically: the unconscious, after gaining a certain amount of energy, sinks back again to its former distance. The final outcome is depressing: human consciousness and life in general suffer an incalculable loss through an incomprehensible *lusus naturae* that lacks all human meaning, a "frolic" on a cosmic scale. This in turn points to something psychic that is not understood by the present. Though the nightmare is over for the survivors, from now on they live in a devastated world. Consciousness has suffered a loss of its own reality, as though the evil dream had robbed it of something essential and made off with it. The loss involved in such a collision consists in missing a unique opportunity, which may never occur again, to come to terms with the contents of the unconscious. Although it was possible to establish an intelligent connection with the cloud, the communication of its contents proved to be unendurable and led to the death of those who submitted to the experiment. Nothing is learnt of the contents from the other side. The encounter with the unconscious ends bootlessly. Our knowledge is not enriched; on this point we remain where we were before the catastrophe. The only thing is that we are at least half a world poorer. The scientific pioneers, the spokesmen of the *avant-garde*, prove too weak or too immature to receive the message from the unconscious. It remains to be seen whether this melancholy outcome is a prophecy or a subjective confession.

If we compare this tale with the *naïvetés* of Angelucci, we get a valuable picture of the difference between the uneducated and the scientifically educated attitude. Both shift the problem into the concrete, the one in order to make us believe in a saving action from heaven, the other in order to transform this secret yet somewhat sinister expectation into an entertaining literary joke. Both, poles apart though they are, are activated by the same unconscious factor and make use of essentially the same symbolism in order to express the unconscious straits we are in.

SUPPLEMENT

An equally recent book, a novel by John Wyndham called *The Midwich Cuckoos* (London and New York, 1957), attributes to a "thing", which is obviously a UFO, a highly significant character. Of unknown but presumably extra-terrestrial origin, this thing casts a spell on a small, remote English village, causing man and beast to fall into an hypnotic sleep which lasts for twenty-four hours. The zone of sleep describes a circle round the village, and any living being that approaches instantly falls asleep when the magical line is crossed. After twenty-four hours everybody revives, and nothing seems to have happened—on the surface. But several weeks later peculiar discoveries are made: first one and then another of the female population, and finally all its members capable of fecundation, are found to be pregnant. In due course children are born with golden eyes. When they develop, they begin to show signs of uncommon intelligence. Later it becomes known that the same miracle has befallen a village in Siberia, an Eskimo settlement, and an African village. In England, owing to the remoteness and insignificance of the locality, the village authorities succeed in hushing up a public scandal. The extraordinary intelligence of the children inevitably leads to trouble and a special school is founded for them. The amazing fact is discovered that, if one of the boys has learnt something new and hitherto unknown, all the boys know it, and the same is true of the girls, so that only one boy and one girl have to attend school. Finally the perspicacious schoolteacher can no longer doubt that the children with golden eyes represent a superior type of Homo sapiens. Their advanced intelligence is, moreover, coupled with a complete realization of their potential power for world domination. The question of how to deal with this menace leads to different solutions. The Africans kill the children immediately. The Eskimos expose them to the cold. The Russians, after isolating the village, destroy it by bombardment. But in England the favourite teacher introduces some boxes, apparently containing laboratory equipment but actually containing dynamite, into the schoolroom and blows himself up with all the children.

The peculiar parthenogenesis and the golden eyes denote kinship with the sun and characterize the children as divine progeny. Their fathers seem to have been angels of the annunciation who had come down from a "supracelestial place" to take care of the stupidity and backwardness of Homo sapiens. It is a divine intervention that gives evolution a definite push forward—or, expressed in more modern terms, an advanced species of man from some other planet visit the earth in order to make biological experiments with mutation and artificial insemination. But the modern Neanderthal man is in no way ready to renounce the prerogatives of the ruling race, and prefers to maintain the status quo by the devastating methods which have always been his final argument.

It is obvious that the sun children, miraculously begotten, represent an unexpected capacity for a wider and higher consciousness, superseding a backward and inferior mental state. Nothing is said, however, about a higher feeling and moral level, which would be necessary to compensate and regulate the possibilities of advanced perception and intellect. Characteristically enough, this aspect does not seem to enter the author's field of vision. It is sufficient for him that the children have a definite advantage of some kind over contemporary man. What if the children should symbolize the germ of some higher potentiality transcending the hitherto valid form of man? In that case the story looks very like a time-honoured repetition of the hero's threatened childhood and his early death through treachery. On the other hand there is something definitely suspect about these children: they are not separated individually but live in a permanent state of *participation mystique*, or unconscious identity, that precludes individual differentiation and development. Had they been spared an early extinction, they would have founded an entirely uniform society, the deadly boredom of which would have been the very ideal of a Marxist state. Thus the negative end of the story remains a matter for doubt.

INDEX

Routledge Classics
Get inside a great mind

Dreams
Carl Gustav Jung

'He taught himself how to read the language of dreams as if they were the forgotten language of the gods themselves.'
Laurens van der Post

In this revolutionary work, the visionary thinker Carl Gustav Jung examines the meaning and function of our dreams and argues that by paying proper attention to them and their significance we can better understand our inner selves. He believed that dreams are the 'most common and most normal expression of the unconscious psyche' and therefore provide the 'bulk of the material for its investigation.' This edition comprises Jung's most important writings on dreams and as an overall survey of the subject it is without parallel.

Hb: 0–415–26740–4   Pb: 0–415–26741–2

Modern Man in Search of a Soul
Carl Gustav Jung

'He was more than a psychological or scientific phenomenon; he was to my mind one of the greatest religious phenomena the world has ever experienced.'
Laurens van der Post

Modern Man in Search of a Soul is the perfect introduction to the theories and concepts of one of the most original and influential religious thinkers of the twentieth century. Lively and insightful, it covers all his most significant themes, including man's need for a God and the mechanics of dream analysis. One of his most famous books, it perfectly captures the feelings of confusion that many sense today.

Hb: 0–415–25544–9   Pb: 0–415–25390–X

For these and other classic titles from Routledge, visit
www.routledgeclassics.com

Some titles not available in North America

Routledge Classics
Get inside a great mind

On the Nature of the Psyche
Carl Gustav Jung

'Next to Freud, no psychiatrist of today has advanced our insight into the nature of the psyche more than Jung has.'
Herman Hesse

Jung's discovery of the 'collective unconscious', a psychic inheritance common to all humankind, transformed the understanding of the self and the way we interpret the world. In *On the Nature of the Psyche*, Jung describes this remarkable theory in his own words, and presents a masterly overview of his theories of the unconscious and its relation to the conscious mind. Also contained in this collection is *On Psychic Energy*, where Jung defends his interpretation of the libido, a key factor in the breakdown of his relations with Freud. For anyone seeking to understand Jung's insights into the human mind, this volume is essential reading.

Hb: 0–415–25545–7   Pb: 0–415–25391–8

The Science of Mythology
Essays on the myth of the divine child and the mysteries of Eleusis
Carl Gustav Jung and Carl Kerényi

'Jung was probably the most significant original thinker of the century.'
Kathleen Raine

This book investigates the authors' contention that an appreciation of mythology is crucial to an understanding of the human mind. It argues that ancient myths were built up from primordial images carried within our unconscious, reflecting ancestral experiences common to us all. Myths surround us today as much as they did in classical times, making this the perfect guide for those who want to unearth their significance and gain an insight into their own predicament.

Hb: 0–415–26743–9   Pb: 0–415–26742–0

For these and other classic titles from Routledge, visit
www.routledgeclassics.com

Routledge Classics
Get inside a great mind

Routledge Classics
Get inside a great mind

Evolution as a Religion
Strange hopes and stranger fears
Mary Midgley

'A graceful, refreshing and enlightening book, applied philosophy that is relevant, timely and metaphysical in the best sense.'
New York Times Book Review

Considered one of Britain's finest philosophers, Midgley exposes the illogical logic of poor doctrines that shelter themselves behind the prestige of science. In *Evolution as a Religion* she examines how science comes to be used as a substitute for religion and points out how badly that role distorts it. As ever, her argument is flawlessly insightful: a punchy, compelling, lively indictment of these misuses of science. Both the book and its author are true classics of our time.

Hb: 0–415–27832–5   Pb: 0–415–27833–3

The Logic of Scientific Discovery
Karl Popper

'One of the most important documents of the twentieth century.'
Peter Medawar, New Scientist

First published in English in 1959, Karl Popper's *The Logic of Scientific Discovery* revolutionized contemporary thinking about science and knowledge and is one of the most widely read books about science written last century. In presenting his now-legendary doctrine of 'falsification', it electrified the scientific community and it now ranks alongside *The Open Society and its Enemies* as one of Popper's most enduring and famous books and contains insights and arguments that demand to be read to this day.

Hb: 0–415–27843–0   Pb: 0–415–27844–9

For these and other classic titles from Routledge, visit
www.routledgeclassics.com

Printed in the United States
by Baker & Taylor Publisher Services